Airfields of the
D-Day Invasion Force

First published in Great Britain in 2009 by
Pen & Sword Aviation
an imprint of
Pen & Sword Books Ltd
47 Church Street
Barnsley
South Yorkshire
S70 2AS

ISBN 978 1 84415 900 0

Printed and bound in the UK
by CPI Ltd

Pen & Sword Books Ltd incorporates the imprints of
Pen & Sword Aviation, Pen & Sword Family History, Pen & Sword Maritime,
Pen & Sword Military, Wharncliffe Local History, Pen & Sword Select,
Pen & Sword Military Classics, Leo Cooper, Remember When,
Seaforth Publishing and Frontline Publishing.

For a complete list of Pen & Sword titles please contact
PEN & SWORD BOOKS LIMITED
47 Church Street, Barnsley, South Yorkshire, S70 2AS, England
E-mail: enquiries@pen-and-sword.co.uk
Website: www.pen-and-sword.co.uk

Airfields of the D-Day Invasion Force

2nd Tactical Air Force in South-East England in World War Two

Peter Jacobs

Pen & Sword
AVIATION

Acknowledgements

Any book such as this could not have been written without the help of a number of people. First of all I would like to offer my thanks to Seb Cox and his staff at the Air Historical Branch; in particular to Graham Day for his help when researching documents and records and to my former RAF colleague, Mary Hudson, for her help with photographs. For many more years than I care to remember, the AHB has been a valuable source of information and I have always found all the staff to be so helpful and supportive. I would also like to thank the staff at the RAF Museum Hendon, the Imperial War Museum and the Public Records Office. The museums and the PRO have been a tremendous source of photographs and records, as have colleagues such as Ken Delve and Peter Green who have allowed me access to their photographs and material over the years. I am truly grateful to all of these individuals for their help and support over the years.

Whilst official sources are always essential, what never ceases to amaze me is just how helpful members of the local public can be. On many occasions I have just turned up in the local area, not knowing the exact location of some of the airfield sites and have had to rely on local knowledge to help me fit the final pieces of the jigsaw. One good example was at Hunsdon. Although I had a reasonable idea of where the former airfield was, I stopped in the village to talk to one of the locals and he was only too keen to pass on to me his local knowledge from many years. His information took me to the Village Council Hall where, by chance, I met the Chairman of the Parish Council, David Gibbs. David and I chatted for a while and he then gave up part of his day to take me to the airfield where he then gave me a wonderful guided tour, passing on his valuable knowledge to help me with my work.

Whilst my experience at Hunsdon was unplanned and I was rather lucky on the day, the power of the internet enabled me to set up a meeting at Friston with Derry Robinson, the owner of Gayles Farm and the former site of the airfield. The time I spent with Derry was truly marvellous. Not only did he give up his time to host my visit and take me around his farm to show me the reminders of the airfield, but the location on top of the South Downs and the view over the Channel and the Seven Sisters Country Park was outstanding. The internet also proved helpful when researching and locating some of the more remote sites. One good example was how Richard Flagg helped me with the site of the former airfield at Horne. I have never met Richard but we have corresponded by e-mail and his precise directions helped me locate the former airfield; in particular, finding the plaque that marks the former site would have proved extremely hard. I have still not met Richard but I owe my thanks to him for his help.

Another farm owner also deserving of a special mention is Lincoln Cranfield and his wife Rachel. I visited the former site of Chailey and found Bower Farm, which marks the site of the former airfield. Lincoln and Rachel proved to be most helpful hosts and my memories of my short insight into dairy farming will always remain with me. Amongst the others I wish to thank in person include David Brook at Deanland. Again this was another one of those unplanned visits and David kindly let me on to the airfield to have a good look around. Whilst I was fortunate to readily gain the cooperation and support of these land owners, I would ask anyone planning to visit these sites to seek prior permission and to respect the fact that these former airfields are, once again, private property. I would also like to thank David McAllister at Dunsfold Park who found the time to host me during my visit and to Danny, one of the security team, for showing me around the areas that extended beyond those normally accessible to the public.

My interest in many of the airfields goes back many years, which has helped me put together an interesting library of research and photos. I visited a number of sites of former airfields whilst researching my previous book *Airfields of 11 Group* and much of the information was valid for this work. My thanks again to Alan Couchman (North Weald), Peter Turner (Manston), David Brocklehurst (Lympne), Marion Creare (Gravesend), Flight Lieutenant Andy Griffin (Kenley), and to the Reverend (Squadron Leader) Andrew Jolly (Biggin Hill).

My interest in one airfield goes back even further. Coolham in Sussex is perhaps unknown to many except the more serious enthusiast or to the local population. I first visited the site back in

1994 for a commemorative weekend, during which I was proudly able to exhibit the medals and logbooks belonging to Squadron Leader 'Wag' Haw, the CO of 129 Squadron at Coolham during the D-Day operations. At the event I met Paul Hamlin, a local policeman, who had spent many years researching the history of Coolham. Along with his committee of volunteers, Paul was responsible for the airfield memorial that has since stood proudly in the village. I have never had the chance to publicly thank Paul for the work that he has done over so many years, until now. Paul Hamlin typifies many locals in villages around the country who have spent many years of their lives ensuring that airfields such as Coolham are never forgotten. I salute Paul and all the others for their dedication and commitment.

Contents

Introduction

This is the second book about airfields that I have had the pleasure to write. The first was about the airfields of No. 11 Group during the Battle of Britain, which I found fascinating to research and write. Now I am able to give you the first of two volumes covering the airfields used by the Second Tactical Air Force (2nd TAF) during the period of the D-Day operations. Whilst D-Day, 6 June 1944, is a date that is familiar to everyone in the history of warfare, the fact that the RAF's 2nd TAF existed may be less well known. The 2nd TAF had formed in November 1943 from an earlier initiative to form a composite organisation to support the Allied invasion of Europe, called Operation *Overlord*. By D-Day it had grown into a mighty air armada, which provided the vital air support to the Allied ground forces as they landed on the beaches of Normandy and then subsequently broke out and advanced towards Germany.

This first volume covers the airfields actively used by 2nd TAF in the south-east of England and the second volume will cover the airfields in the south and south-west of England. Because of the number of airfields and landing grounds in West Sussex, the western boundary I have used to differentiate between the two volumes is a line running due south from Guildford to just east of Bognor Regis. Airfields and landing grounds to the east of this line are included in this first volume. Those lying to the west will be covered in the next volume.

It is worth noting that not all the airfields covered in this first volume were used during the air operations on D-Day itself but they were used by 2nd TAF during the period November 1943 to June 1944; therefore, they are included for completeness. Whilst this volume covers the airfields and landing grounds in the south-east of England, I have also included the airfields just to the north of London and in East Anglia. Again this is for completeness otherwise these airfields would be a glaring omission from the full story. This means that a total of twenty-six airfields are covered in this volume, although in fact some were developed as Advanced Landing Grounds (ALGs) rather than being given full airfield status.

These landing grounds in southern England had been identified as early as 1942 to become temporary airfields for the large number of British and American squadrons for a limited period of time to support the Allied invasion of Europe. Each landing ground was constructed to a similar pattern: two metal track runways (up to 1,600 yards long and fifty yards wide), a perimeter track and aircraft standings on more metal tracking, up to eight blister hangars and a facility for storing fuel. Some of these landing grounds, such as Brenzett, Lydd, New Romney and Swingfield, were either inactive during 1944 or held in reserve, and so these are not included in this work. Others were handed to the US Ninth Air Force during early 1944 and so were under American command and control during the period leading up to, and during, the D-Day operations. These landing grounds, which include Ashford, Headcorn, High Halden, Kingsnorth, Lashenden, Staplehurst and Woodchurch, are also not included in this work.

Because of the large number of airfields, I have chosen to cover them in alphabetical order within geographical chapters, starting with the airfields north of London and in East Anglia, and then work in a clockwise direction through Greater London, Kent, Sussex and finally Surrey. First though, to put the story behind each airfield's contribution to 2nd TAF into some context, I have given an insight into the formation of 2nd TAF and then given a summary of D-Day itself. The two Appendices provide 2nd TAF's order of battle at the time of its formation and then on D-Day itself.

Whilst this book focuses on events during late 1943 and the first six months of 1944, each airfield has its history before and after its time with 2nd TAF and I have included brief historical details of each airfield to give a greater understanding of what went on before and after 1944. I have also given details of some of the gallant airmen that operated from these airfields during this period as it is the people that make the history of the airfield so fascinating. Many of these were decorated fighter pilots and I have used the correct abbreviation when referring to their awards. The abbreviation DSO stands for the Distinguished Service Order, DFC is the Distinguished Flying Cross and DFM is the Distinguished Flying Medal. After the history of each airfield I have provided a summary of the squadrons that served at the airfield during the latter months of 1943 up to the summer of 1944.

The origins of some of the more famous airfields covered in this volume, such as Biggin Hill and Kenley, date back to the First World

War. The reason for this is quite straightforward as the south-east of England, with its close proximity to London, witnessed the birth of military aviation in Britain. After the First World War there often developed a similar pattern for many of these airfields as the RAF's history unfolded. Other airfields, however, remain largely unheard of and places such as Chailey, Coolham, Deanland and Friston may not be so familiar. Some of these sites offer few, if any, reminders of their existence as airfields in 1944 whereas others proudly remember the past with memorials funded and erected locally. I usually find these sites more interesting to visit than some of the others that have since become major international airports. For example, the contrast between Gatwick and Horne, which are just a few miles apart, is quite staggering. It took me some time to find the former site of Horne and I eventually came across a plaque in a position marking the corner of the former airfield. On the other hand Gatwick is signposted from the M25 and provides no challenge in navigation whatsoever. But if I had to return to just one of the two sites to reflect on the past it would be Horne without any doubt.

Where these places and landmarks exist I have given directions to help find them and I hope you will find these of use if planning to visit any of the sites. I have visited every site and only time and space prevents me from writing more but, once again, researching and, more importantly, visiting all these sites has proved to be a fascinating experience. I hope you think so too.

Air Chief Marshal Sir Trafford Leigh-Mallory, commander of the Allied Expeditionary Air Force (AEAF)

CHAPTER 1

2nd Tactical Air Force

As the political and military leaders made preparations for the Allied invasion of mainland Europe, called Operation *Overlord*, it became increasingly evident that tactical air power would be pivotal to success. This led to the existence of two great, and well equipped, tactical air forces to support the invasion; these were the United States Ninth Air Force and the RAF's Second Tactical Air Force (2nd TAF) with both air forces under the command of Air Chief Marshal Sir Trafford Leigh-Mallory. In addition to these tactical air forces, the Supreme Commander of the Allied Forces, General Dwight D. Eisenhower, had the use of RAF Bomber Command and the United States Eighth Air Force.

The RAF's 2nd TAF had grown out of an early initiative during 1943 to form a composite organisation to support the planned Allied invasion of Europe. The need for re-organisation within the RAF's structure came about as the direction of the Second World War moved from a defensive posture to an offensive one. With the battles of France and Britain over, the RAF went increasingly on the offensive and by the beginning of 1943, the pilots of Fighter Command had become familiar with flying fighter sweeps over enemy-occupied territory.

The aim of the fighter sweep missions was often to encourage the *Luftwaffe* into the air but this tactic rarely worked and so the RAF's fighters took to escorting the light/medium bombers on raids against enemy targets in a further attempt to encourage the *Luftwaffe*'s fighters into the air. The range of the RAF fighters was limited and so, again, this tactic had limited success. However, what had become obvious was that Fighter Command's role to defend the homeland had all but come to an end. Furthermore, as the war progressed through 1943 there were a number of changes made to the structure and organisation of the RAF. This was brought about for various reasons but one of the key factors was because Britain and her Allies were now fighting side by side in the North-West Europe theatre.

In 1943 Fighter Command, Bomber Command and Coastal Command were still generally doing their own thing but in terms of supporting forces on the ground there had at that stage of the war been little in the way of joint operations between the RAF and the Army. The only organisation regularly involved in such support was Army Cooperation Command. This Command had been formed at the end of 1940 as the complexity and diversity of air power started to increase. Army Cooperation Command controlled two groups: No. 70 Group for training and No. 71 Group as the operational force. Whilst units involved with the Command often tired of the endless number of exercises, their tactics and techniques developed during 1942 and early 1943 would later prove invaluable, although the Command itself was disbanded in June 1943 as part of the re-organisation of tactical air power.

Whilst air support of ground operations was limited at home to conducting numerous exercises, the same could not be said in North Africa where air and land forces had fought in harmony. The ultimate victory in North Africa brought two key factors to the Allied table. Firstly, assets and resources were made available for use elsewhere and secondly, vast tactical experience had been gained in the desert; the Western Desert Air Force had supported the British Eighth Army and the North-West African Air Force had supported the British First Army. Following victory these two air forces were merged to form the Desert Air Force, or the First Tactical Air Force, to take part in operations during the invasion of Southern Europe. The experience gained in North Africa, and the formation of a First Tactical Air Force, soon led to discussions to form a Second Tactical Air Force, which would conduct operations in support of the planned invasion of Western Europe.

The disbandment of Army Cooperation Command in 1943 saw its units transferred to Fighter Command, about the same time that the light/medium day bombers of No. 2 Group Bomber Command had also been transferred to Fighter Command. Two new groups had also been formed within Fighter Command during 1943; No. 83 Group at Redhill on 1 April under the command of Air

Vice-Marshal William Dickson, and No. 84 Group at Cowley Barracks, Oxford, on 15 July under the command of Air Commodore Theodore McEvoy. These three new groups within Fighter Command would later form the basis of 2nd TAF. No. 83 Group and No. 84 Group were detailed to support the Second British Army and First Canadian Army respectively; both were major elements of the 21st Army Group, which was the British and Commonwealth contribution to the main Allied invasion force of Western Europe.

The most significant change to the higher level structure came on 13 November 1943 with the formation of the Allied Expeditionary Air Force (AEAF), under the command of Air Chief Marshal Sir Trafford Leigh-Mallory, with its Headquarters at Stanmore Park. Now fifty-one years old, Leigh-Mallory had commanded No. 12 Group during the Battle of Britain. He had survived the post-Battle of Britain shuffle of commanders and took command of No. 11 Group in November 1941. Promoted to the rank of air marshal a year later he then replaced William Sholto Douglas as head of Fighter Command. Both Sholto Douglas and Leigh-Mallory were instrumental in developing the strategy that would take the RAF through the rest of the war. They both had the support of the Chief of the Air Staff, Charles Portal. Sholto Douglas believed in the concept of the 'Big Wing' and Leigh-Mallory believed that there should be a single commander of an Allied Air Force, rather than a number of different commanders all at the same rank, who would have overall command of individual commands such as Fighter Command and Bomber Command; therefore, how fitting it should be that Leigh-Mallory was appointed as the first commander of the AEAF.

When the AEAF formed it had three components. One was the United States Ninth Air Force, which had been formed in the Mediterranean just three months before and had moved to England on 10 September. On 15 November the other two components were formed when Fighter Command disbanded; its non-tactical units reverted to the pre-1936 title of Air Defence of Great Britain (ADGB) as the second component of the AEAF, and its tactical units became 2nd TAF as the third component.

The first commander of 2nd TAF was Air Marshal Arthur Coningham, although Coningham would not return to the UK to assume his command until 10 January 1944. Born in Australia but

The first commander of 2nd TAF was Air Marshal Arthur Coningham (right). He and the Deputy Supreme Allied Commander, Sir Arthur Tedder (left), had previously worked closely together during the air campaign in the desert.

brought up in New Zealand, Coningham had served in the First World War as a soldier before joining the Royal Flying Corps. By the end of hostilities he had been credited with nineteen kills and had been awarded the DSO, Military Cross and the DFC. He remained in the post-war RAF, serving in various appointments, and at the outbreak of the Second World War he was AOC No. 4 Group. Coningham was, indeed, a natural choice as commander of 2nd TAF. He had previously commanded the Western Desert Air Force during 1942 and had championed the development of tactical air support for Allied troops on the ground. His leadership had been inspirational during the victory in North Africa and he subsequently directed tactical operations during the invasion of Sicily and Italy.

When 2nd TAF formed in November 1943, the three groups within its organisation were Nos 2, 83 and 84 Groups. AOC No. 2 Group was Air Vice-Marshal Basil Embry who had held the appointment since 1 June 1943. Embry had joined the RAF as a pilot in 1921 at the age of just nineteen and would later become a legend as one of only two members of the Service to be awarded four DSOs; the other was Wing Commander 'Willie' Tait, leader of the famous raid against the German battleship *Tirpitz*. By the time Embry took up appointment as AOC No. 2 Group he had been awarded two bars to the DSO he had earned on the North-West Frontier of India before the Second World War; both bars were earned in 1940 whilst commanding No. 107 Squadron at Wattisham. The first was for leading an attack by twelve Blenheims against Stavanger airfield in Norway during April 1940 and the second was for supporting ground troops in France and the Low Countries during the evacuation at Dunkirk just a few weeks later. Embry was then due for a rest from operations and was about to take up appointment as the Station Commander at West Raynham but on his last operational sortie he was shot down by ground fire. Having baled out of his burning Blenheim behind enemy lines, Embry was captured by the Germans and was taken away as a prisoner of war. However, he was lucky and an opportune moment allowed him to make his escape. Embry evaded capture for two months and made his way towards Spain. He was briefly captured once more, this time by the Vichy French, but managed to escape for a second time and he eventually made his way to Gibraltar. He finally arrived back in the UK and he then took up various senior appointments, including time at HQ Desert Air Force, before he was appointed AOC No. 2 Group. Embry would remain as AOC until the end of the war but he took whatever opportunity he had to fly on operations; his gallantry in action brought him a third bar to his DSO and a DFC during the final weeks of the war.

William Dickson initially remained as AOC No. 83 Group but he soon handed over to Air Vice-Marshal Harry Broadhurst. When Broadhurst was appointed as AOC No. 83 Group he had only just turned thirty-eight, which made him the youngest air vice-marshal in the RAF. The son of an Army officer, Broadhurst had initially followed his father's career by joining the Army in 1925. However, he wanted to fly and so he transferred to the RAF just a year later. After pilot training, Broadhurst initially served in India and received a Mention in Despatches for his services on the North-West Frontier. Once back home he quickly gained a reputation as an accomplished instructor and aerobatic display pilot, and he was awarded the Air Force Cross in 1937. During the early years of the Second World War Broadhurst flew Hurricanes and Spitfires with Fighter Command, first as a squadron commander and then as a station commander. By the time he was posted to the Western Desert in late 1942 he had been credited with thirteen confirmed kills for which he had been awarded the DSO and bar, and a DFC and bar. Broadhurst then assumed command as AOC Western Desert, taking over from his new 2nd TAF superior, Arthur Coningham. Whilst in the desert, Broadhurst managed to commandeer a captured Fiesler Storch aircraft; he had the aircraft painted in British markings and used it for touring the units under his command.

By the middle of November 1943 command of No. 84 Group had been handed over from Theodore McEvoy to Air Vice-Marshal Leslie Brown. At the time of his appointment as AOC No. 84 Group, Brown was fifty years old. Born in South Africa he had served as a pilot in the Royal Naval Air Service (RNAS) during the First World War. Brown had gained valuable experience of joint operations during the inter-war years, in particular during the mid-late 1930s when he served on the Air Staff at HQ 22 (Army Cooperation) Group after which he was given command of No. 50 (Army Cooperation) Wing. Prior to his appointment as AOC, Brown had previously served in the Middle East when he had been instrumental in helping build up the Desert Air Force.

There was no doubting the fact that the leadership of 2nd TAF was very strong, although the relationship between some of the senior British officers in major appointments during the build up to Operation *Overlord* could make an interesting discussion. However, from 2nd TAF's point of view, things were looking up and by that stage of the war the commanders of the numerous wings and squadrons were generally full of experience; it was, to say the least, an impressive line-up.

Not only were there changes to the hierarchy but there were also changes at the lower level of organisation as well. By the time 2nd TAF was being formed the airfields had been numbered. For example, Biggin Hill had become No. 126 Airfield and Kenley had become No. 127 Airfield; it did not matter whether the airfield was

Some airfields, as well as the Advanced Landing Grounds, were not capable of supporting operations all year round and in adverse weather. The solution was for engineers to lay metal strips for runways, known as Sommerfield tracks.

a main RAF base or of satellite status. In addition, the airfields had been 'paired up' to form wings. Using the same example of Biggin Hill and Kenley, these two airfields were paired together to initially form No. 17 Fighter Wing. The concept of numbered airfields did not last long following the formation of 2nd TAF and a wing system was adopted. For example, Kenley, previously No. 127 Airfield, became No. 127 Wing and Sculthorpe, previously No. 140 Airfield, became No. 140 Wing.

The number of squadrons at each base varied, from one in the case of smaller airfields to three at the larger bases. Although each squadron retained its aircraft and aircrew, the ground crews were often assigned to the airfield or wing, rather than to an individual squadron. Understandably, this concept was not particularly popular amongst all the ground crew as many enjoyed feeling that they were part of the squadron. This was a bond that carried pilots and ground crews through the Battle of Britain and for three years after; indeed, it has remained an important factor up to the present day.

At the time of its formation in November 1943, the Headquarters of 2nd TAF was at Hartford Bridge and it had been assigned a total of fifty-six squadrons. The largest of its three groups, in terms of the number of squadrons, was No. 83 Group, which had twenty front-line squadrons spread across eight airfields at: Biggin Hill, Kenley, Westhampnett, Gravesend, Detling, Gatwick, Merston and Redhill. In addition, the group had units from four observation squadrons (Auster IIIs) attached to various airfields. The second largest group was No. 84 Group with sixteen front-line squadrons spread across seven airfields at: Hornchurch, Northolt, Heston, Ibsley, Odiham, Thruxton and Perranporth. There were also units from three observation squadrons attached to various airfields. The smallest of the groups in terms of the number of squadrons was No. 2 Group, which had eleven squadrons at five airfields: Hartford Bridge, Sculthorpe, Swanton Morley, Dunsfold and Lasham. There were also two squadrons of Spitfires (IVs and XIs) at Hartford Bridge assigned to the Headquarters. Full details of the airfields and squadrons of 2nd TAF at the time of its formation are at Appendix One.

A number of different RAF fighter aircraft types were involved in operations at that time. For example, squadrons with the role of ensuring air superiority by attacking enemy fighters used the Spitfire IXs and fighter-bomber squadrons specialising in ground-attack operated Typhoon IAs. Essentially the squadrons of Nos 83 and 84 Groups were equipped with Spitfires (Vs and IXs), Mustangs (Is and IAs), Hurricane IVs and Typhoon IAs, whilst No. 2 Group operated Mitchell IIs, Boston IIIs and Mosquito VIs. The types of operations flown by the squadrons were given names such as *Rodeos* for fighter raids over enemy territory, *Rhubarbs* for low-level fighter attacks on targets of convenience, *Circus* for escorting medium-bombers and *Ramrod* for protecting heavy bombers.

The fourth component of 2nd TAF, No. 85 Group, formed at Uxbridge on 17 December 1943. A few weeks later Air Vice-Marshal J.B. Cole-Hamilton was appointed as AOC No. 85 Group. This group differed from the others in 2nd TAF in that it was formed to adopt a defensive posture with the main roles of providing air defence over the invasion build-up areas along the south coast of England and night defence of the 2nd TAF airfields. The plan was that once the invasion started to take place then No. 85 Group would continue to provide night air defence over the Army's front-line units. The group was, therefore, equipped with Mosquito XIII night-fighters and high-altitude Spitfires (VIIs and XIVs) to combat the enemy's high-altitude reconnaissance aircraft and detailed to over-fly the likely invasion ports along the south coast of England.

During the early weeks of 1944 there was no great change to the flying for the squadron pilots with offensive sweeps and attacks against German targets in occupied territory being the norm. However, increasingly the squadrons began taking part in exercises with ground forces. There was also a build-up of newer aircraft types such as later variants of the Spitfire, the Typhoon and the Mustang.

Coningham was an experienced commander of large forces of many aircraft types. Over the next few months, as the Allies prepared to launch their invasion of mainland Europe, his new air force would grow to more than 100 squadrons based at some fifty airfields. Many of these airfields would be temporary and poorly equipped, and were scattered all across southern England. By D-Day there would be some 11,000 aircraft available of which more than 4,000 were British and nearly 7,000 were American. The Allies would have more than 4,000 heavy bombers, 1,000 medium and light bombers, about 4,500 fighters and nearly 1,000 troop-carrying aircraft; the remainder was made up of reconnaissance aircraft and air-sea rescue aircraft.

In preparing his force for what was to come, Coningham was keen to impress on his personnel that they were part of a mobile force with the task of supporting the forces on the ground. The experience he had gained on the Western Front during the First World War, and in the Western Desert during the earlier years of the Second World War, stood him in good stead for turning his Air Force into a mobile and expeditionary one. There should be no thoughts along the lines of being static because, once the invasion was under way, he knew that his force would, in his words, become a 'travelling circus'. Therefore, he did not want his personnel to become 'too comfortable' at their bases and so many thousands were denied the comforts of permanent accommodation at the airfields and were given tents instead; they were also instructed to set up temporary accommodation and facilities around the edges of the airfields. And so in early 1944, during the hard winter months, the men and women of 2nd TAF found out just what being part of a mobile force was all about.

Armourers preparing a Typhoon prior to another mission during the winter of 1943/4. Originally intended to be a replacement for the Hurricane, the Typhoon evolved into one of the Second World War's most successful ground-attack aircraft.

The Mustang proved a valuable asset to 2nd TAF

In addition to the reorganisation on the ground, the training for the fighter pilots changed as well. There was less training in dogfighting, the fighter pilot's natural skill, but more and more training in air-to-ground gunnery as well as introducing more and more training in air-to-ground rocket attacks and low-level bombing. It was not that Coningham considered air-to-air fighting unimportant but he was satisfied that by early 1944 the majority of fighter pilots were comfortable, indeed many were very experienced, in air-to-air combat but very few had been trained in air-ground weaponry; this was to be vital in the coming weeks and months if air support to the Allied invasion was to be a success.

As soon as Coningham arrived back in the UK to take up his new command he set up an Advanced Headquarters at Uxbridge, which was close enough for him to attend meetings at the AEAF HQ at Bentley Priory and his Main HQ at Bracknell. By all accounts the HQ at Uxbridge ran 'like clockwork' with everyone fully aware of their task and what was expected of them. Those under his

The use of metal tracking gave the airfields and Advanced Landing Grounds the capability of operating throughout the winter of 1943/44.

command considered Coningham to be an outstanding operational commander. He knew how to get the best from his staff and, as importantly, worked extremely well with the Army and the Americans; furthermore, he was well respected by both. Coningham was said to have always been in control and never dithered nor panicked. He was, by all accounts, the ideal commander during the vital period leading up to the invasion. He not only involved himself with the strategic aspects of his command, at the very highest levels, but he also got out and about to the various airfields and sites so that he could meet the personnel under his command in order to gain a full appreciation of what the situation was like at the lower levels of his command.

Coningham attended a particularly important meeting at Bentley Priory at the end of April when Leigh-Mallory established the responsibilities of the different Air HQs during the invasion; Leigh-Mallory would, himself, coordinate the strategic and tactical elements of the air battle. However, once the battle was underway, Coningham would not only command 2nd TAF but he would also command the Advanced AEAF HQ until Leigh-Mallory could establish himself in France. During May 1944 the senior commanders continued to meet at Bentley Priory to decide the priorities of the strategic targets and to agree the effort and responsibilities of the strategic and tactical forces.

As D-Day approached 2nd TAF took deliberate action to destroy the German's radar chain along the northern coast of France. There were too many sites to attack and destroy all of them but if the Allies could neutralise as many as possible then it would enable them to gain the element of surprise during the crucial early hours of D-Day itself. To do this it was decided to use a mix of attack aircraft (mainly rocket-armed Typhoons as well as Typhoons and Spitfires carrying bombs), and radio countermeasures. The role of the sites varied and not all radars could be jammed and so a target list was drawn up with the sites presenting the biggest threat listed as priorities. Attacks took place from mid-May onwards and proved successful; at least six of the German's long-range reporting sites were put out of action and more than a dozen other sites were severely damaged to the point that they were unserviceable on D-Day.

On 4 June all the 2nd TAF aircraft, as well as those of the US Ninth Air Force, were painted with the famous black and white stripe invasion markings. This would help identify friendly aircraft over the beaches once the Allied invasion was underway. Aircraft were ordered not to fly close to enemy territory so that the markings could not be seen, which would have highlighted to the Germans the Allied intent. This made air operations particularly difficult given that the invasion was subsequently postponed for a further twenty-four hours. However, 2nd TAF was now ready to provide the vital air support for the greatest invasion in the history of warfare.

Facilities at the Advanced Landing Grounds were usually very basic and planning had to take place wherever possible.

CHAPTER 2

D-Day

By the time the Allied forces were ready to commence Operation *Overlord* there had assembled a vast organisation of air assets, the command and control aspects of which appear quite complex. There were the airfields of 2nd TAF, which accommodated the bomber units of No. 2 Group, the fighter and fighter-bomber units of No. 83 Group and No. 84 Group, and the day-fighter and night-fighter units of No. 85 Group. The No. 83 Group and No. 84 Group assets were essentially based at airfields stretching along the south coast, mainly in the counties of West Sussex and Hampshire. No. 85 Group assets were spread across the south and south-east, and the bombers of No. 2 Group, with greater range and endurance, which were located inland.

In addition to 2nd TAF were the tactical units of the US Ninth Air Force, the other tactical organisation providing a vast array of air power, most of which were located at airfields in Kent. There were also the fighter squadrons of No. 11 Group ADGB in the south-east, which were located mainly in Kent and Sussex. In addition to all these air assets in the south-east there were additional forces stretching all along the south coast as far as Cornwall and as far north as the East Midlands.

In terms of the number of squadrons, the overall Allied strength totalled 630 squadrons; 254 were British and 376 American. Of the British effort, 100 squadrons were available to 2nd TAF with the remainder being units of Bomber Command and ADGB. Of the American effort, just less than half were available to the US Ninth Air Force with the remainder being units from the US Eighth Air Force.

Intelligence officers played a vital part during the build up to D-Day, and during the period immediately after, to help commanders determine the key targets for the air-to-ground operations in support of Operation *Overlord* and the subsequent Allied breakout from Normandy.

On D-Day the Allies flew a total of more than 3,300 sorties. More than 1,500 fighter sorties were flown over the invasion area, and particularly over the beachhead as the Allied troops went ashore; this included up to 100 fighters at any one time providing fighter cover directly over the beaches during the hours of daylight. The other 1,800 sorties were flown by bombers or fighters providing escort for troop-carrying aircraft or gliders.

The first 2nd TAF aircraft arrived over the planned invasion area at first light, which was around 5.00 a.m. One of the first tasks was to lay a continuous smoke screen over the invasion area and this was carried out by two Boston squadrons from Hartford Bridge. The first Allied landing craft went ashore just before 7.30 a.m. as the fighter-bomber units attacked a number of known defences along

The ground crew worked extremely hard during the period leading up to D-Day.

the landing beaches, many of which were hardened. There were also a number of tactical reconnaissance sorties flown over the landing beaches and immediate inland areas.

During the early and mid-morning there was little air-to-air activity between the Allied fighters and the *Luftwaffe*. This was for a number of reasons. First the *Luftwaffe* units were spread as the actual invasion area had not been worked out by the Germans; furthermore, there was initially, and understandably, much confusion amongst the German High Command during the early hours of the invasion. Secondly, many of the *Luftwaffe* fighter units in Normandy had been withdrawn further away from the coast as the continuous shelling and bombing of specific targets by the Allies during the previous weeks had undoubtedly had an effect.

Thirdly, there was the poor weather on the day. That said, the *Luftwaffe* did manage to put fighters over the invasion area during the morning of 6 June and as the day progressed the *Luftwaffe* did enjoy some success with about twenty Allied aircraft shot down during the course of the day. One notable success for the *Luftwaffe* occurred around midday when Typhoons from Thorney Island that were carrying out a ground-attack mission against tanks to the south of Caen were attacked by Focke-Wulf FW190s; unfortunately for the Typhoons the FW190s came out on top and three Typhoon pilots were shot down and killed.

Like his senior colleagues, Coningham expected the *Luftwaffe* to respond immediately and with great strength to the Allied landings. From his perspective, the lack of aerial opposition during the morning of the invasion was a great bonus but, as the day wore on, the amount of cloud over the invasion area made the task of preventing the enemy's movement on the ground almost impossible. Although German movements towards the invasion area could not be stopped, the presence of rocket-armed Typhoons patrolling over the roads and countryside certainly hampered movements on the ground and delayed much support reaching the German front line until after dark.

Although not of particularly good quality, this aerial photo shows one of the invasion beaches during Operation *Overlord*.

As the air activity intensified during the afternoon, the RAF squadrons destroyed at least seven enemy aircraft and claimed many more as either probably destroyed or damaged. The Spitfire IX squadrons enjoyed the most success, claiming four aircraft destroyed and four more probably destroyed or at least damaged. Only one Spitfire IX was lost to enemy action, in this case the aircraft was hit by flak, but the pilot managed to bale out into the Channel and survived. The Typhoon I squadrons had mixed success as far as the air-to-air battle was concerned, destroying two aircraft during the late afternoon and early evening but with the loss of two Typhoon pilots. The same was true of the Mustang III squadrons; two claims for the loss of one pilot.

During the early evening the second wave of airborne troops crossed the Channel in gliders towed by tugs, which were escorted by 2nd TAF Mustangs. The gliders crossed the coast soon after 9.00 p.m. when they were attacked by Focke-Wulf FW190s. But the escorting Mustangs managed to hold the attackers off, claiming two FW190s during the engagement.

Overall, the day had gone reasonably well for most of the ground forces. In the British Sector the landings at Gold Beach were going well but less so at Juno Beach where the rough sea had caused problems and many of the German defences had still been intact. Also, in the area between Juno and Sword Beaches the German Panzers had mounted a strong counter-attack, although this had been opposed with some success by British airborne forces.

Once darkness had fallen it was the turn of the bombers of No. 2 Group to conduct a number of night raids against road and rail junctions and for the Mosquitos of No. 85 Group to carry out night intruder missions. Bomber Command also flew more than 1,000 sorties against various communications targets to add to the 1,200 sorties it had flown against coastal batteries the night before. This continuous round-the-clock air assault prevented the Germans from moving forces into key positions and prevented any significant counter-attack during the opening twenty-four hours of the Allied invasion.

As daylight broke on the following morning of 7 June, the Allied task was to secure its foothold in Normandy and to widen its bridgehead to allow further reinforcements and then to push forward in an attempt to break out from the beachhead into northern France. There was still some doubt amongst senior

German commanders as to whether this was the main Allied invasion that had long been expected, or not.

As the Allies started to break out from the beachhead, the 2nd TAF squadrons were in continuous demand from first light. For the tactical reconnaissance squadrons there were an increasing number of specific areas to be reported on. This then led to an increased number of sorties by the ground-attack Typhoons to provide the vital support to the Allied forces on the ground. There were, however, increased Allied air losses from the previous day, mainly as a result of increased German ground defences; 2nd TAF alone lost thirty-six aircraft during the day and the Americans suffered even heavier losses. That said, the Allied pilots had also scored considerable success; 2nd TAF pilots claimed more than thirty enemy aircraft destroyed.

One of the Allies' immediate priorities in and around the beachhead was to construct landing strips for fighters. Personnel and equipment from the airfield construction wings were amongst the many to go ashore on 7 June. The construction of landing strips happened in order of operational priority. Construction initially focussed on Emergency Landing Strips for Allied aircraft in

A Typhoon clearly showing the D-Day invasion markings of black and white stripes. The stripes were applied on the fuselage and wings just two days before D-Day.

2nd TAF had seventeen Mosquito squadrons of various marks available to it during June 1944.

desperate need of somewhere to land, followed by the construction of Refuelling and Re-Arming Strips, for quick turn-rounds of aircraft and then Advanced Landing Grounds (ALGs). Once the ALGs had been constructed it was possible to move the operational wings across the Channel from their operating bases along the south coast of England.

The requirement for an ALG was a runway strip of between 1,000 yards and 1,700 yards in length depending on the type of aircraft that were destined to operate from there. The runway surfaces were generally constructed of SMT (square mesh track), which had been developed because the Sommerfield track, used when ALGs had first been constructed in southern England, had caused problems.

On 8 June the story of the air battle was much the same, although the number of claims by 2nd TAF pilots was less than the previous day, so were their losses. The weather then deteriorated during the early hours of 9 June, which brought a significant reduction in Allied sorties flown and at times effectively brought air operations to a halt. By the evening, however, the weather had picked up sufficiently for night operations to take place.

For the first seventy-two hours the effort by the air and ground crews back at the RAF's invasion airfields never ceased. Understandably it was an all-out effort but, equally

Ground crew and Typhoon just after D-Day.

understandably, it could not be sustained indefinitely. Furthermore, Coningham was not entirely sure of the enemy's intent. For some period after the Allied landing in Normandy had begun, many in the German High Command still believed that the main Allied effort was still to come in the Pas de Calais. Although losses to the *Luftwaffe* had been light, many RAF aircraft had been destroyed or damaged by accurate German fire from the ground, as well as from some inaccurate Allied fire in support of the invasion. Until Coningham was able to establish more accurate and reliable information, so that he could more clearly determine the enemy's intent as far as the air battle was concerned, he allowed a brief period of rest for his pilots and to give time for the ground crews to carry out some much needed repairs and maintenance.

As the Allied advance started to gather momentum 2nd TAF aircraft were able to start using the landing strips that were beginning to appear. However, progress on the ground had often been slow due to determined resistance by German forces, which in turn prevented the rapid construction of ALGs. That said, the first landing ground, B.1 at Asnelles-sur-Mer, just inland from Gold Beach, had been completed in remarkably quick time and was available as an emergency landing ground within forty-eight hours of the first troops going ashore.

During detailed planning for the overall air plan earlier in 1944, the Allied planners had hoped that by D+3 (D-Day + 3 days) there would be four Refuelling and Re-Arming Strips, by D+10 it was hoped there would be ten ALGs (five British and five American), by D+14 there would be eighteen ALGs (ten British and eight American) and by D+24 there would be twenty-seven (fifteen British and twelve American). The reality when the invasion came

Three of the RAF's senior commanders in discussion during the D-Day operations: left is Air Marshal Sir Arthur Coningham (Commander 2nd TAF); in the centre is Air Vice-Marshal Harry Broadhurst (AOC No. 83 Group); and Air Chief Marshal Sir Arthur Tedder (Deputy Supreme Allied Commander) is on the right.

was somewhat different. Delays in consolidating and then expanding the bridgehead prevented vital equipment and personnel going ashore. By D+10, 16 June, instead of there being ten ALGs there were six complete, and by D+19 the number had risen to eleven rather than the twenty planned.

Coningham was obviously keen to get his shorter-ranged aircraft operating from across the Channel as soon as possible if he was to establish, and maintain, early air superiority in the skies over the invasion area. Furthermore, an attack by V-1 flying bombs against London on the night of 15/16 June meant that seven 2nd TAF squadrons were taken out of the immediate support for the invasion to assist the RAF's efforts against the V-1 sites as part of Operation *Crossbow*.

Once established across the Channel, there were the occasional periods of relaxation between sorties but generally the operational tempo remained high throughout the Allied breakout of Normandy.

Whilst this slower than hoped progress caused some concern to the Allied commanders, it never became a critical issue as eventually there would be 220 airfields constructed in north-west Europe (150 British and seventy American). The numbering of these airfields was quite simple; the British airfields were 'B-numbered' in sequence, for example B.56 was at Evere, and the American airfields were 'A-numbered' in sequence, for example A.56 was at Crecey.

By the end of June 1944 nearly one million troops and equipment had gone ashore in Normandy. Operation *Epsom*, the plan to capture Caen and the surrounding countryside, which would be vital to the construction of airfields, began on 25 June. Strong German resistance in the region led to follow-up efforts, Operation *Charnwood* launched on 7 July, and Operation *Goodwood* on 18 July. Slowly the Allies managed to make a breakout. Coningham gave the role of maintaining air superiority ahead of pursuing columns and providing close air support to No. 83 Group, which was operating with the 2nd British Army. He gave No. 84 Group, which was working with the 1st Canadian Army, the task of protecting the western flank of the advance as well as providing support to combined operations required to capture the ports between Le Havre and Antwerp.

On 5 August Coningham reverted to command 2nd TAF as the Advanced AEAF was no longer required and ceased to exist. He was now able to move his HQ across the Channel to Le Tronquay to the south of Bayeux. As the Allied forces advanced, more and more airfields were captured and, once cleared of hazards and booby traps, these airfields were in turn used by the Allies. As the advance gathered pace, Coningham moved his HQ first to Amiens and then to Brussels. By the end of September the Allies came up against the natural barriers of the major rivers, which for the time being prevented further advance.

With Allied forces safely established on mainland Europe, and with the renewed threat to southern England from opportunity raids by the *Luftwaffe*, and the continued attacks against London by the V-1 flying bombs, the decision was taken to re-form Fighter Command and the interception of V-1s became one of the Command's key responsibilities. This took place on 15 October 1944 and ADGB vanished once more.

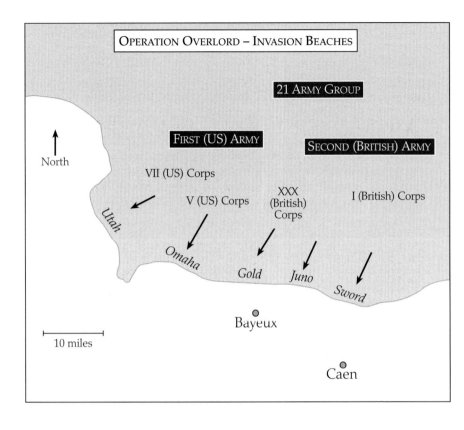

CHAPTER 3

Airfields of Essex, Hertfordshire and East Anglia

East Anglia and its surrounding counties have a long association with the history of aviation. Balloon flights reportedly took place from the region more than 200 years ago and the area was involved with development and experimentation during the early days of powered flight. The landscape of the region varies from very flat land, which is often very wet in the Fens, to undulating hills. Whilst much of the land was not suitable for aviation, there were nonetheless parts of the region where the land offered firm foundations for the construction of airfields.

When the Second World War broke out there were some twenty military airfields and landing grounds in East Anglia. By 1945 the number had increased to more than 100 such was the rapid expansion in the number of airfields in this region during the war. The greatest expansion period was during the latter half of 1942 and early 1943 as more American units crossed the Atlantic to participate in the war in Europe. The overall construction effort was enormous.

For aviation enthusiasts and modern day historians, the airfields of East Anglia and its surrounding counties offer great variety in terms of the numbers and types of aircraft that operated from them during the war. The vast majority of the region's airfields have long disappeared with much of the land being reverted to agriculture.

As far as the region's involvement with 2nd TAF is concerned, particularly during the period leading up to and during the Allied invasion of Europe, there were only a handful of airfields actively involved in terms of flying operations. The reason for this is quite straightforward; the airfields of East Anglia and its surrounding counties were considerably further from the planned invasion area than those airfields along the south coast and given the limited range and endurance of the 2nd TAF fighters it is fully understandable that these aircraft were deployed further south in the period leading up to the invasion.

Therefore, this chapter concentrates on just five airfields: Bradwell Bay and North Weald in Essex, Hunsdon in Hertfordshire, and Sculthorpe and Swanton Morley in Norfolk. Whilst only Hunsdon was actively involved in operations across the Channel on D-Day, the other airfields were used during the preparation period and are, therefore, included for completeness.

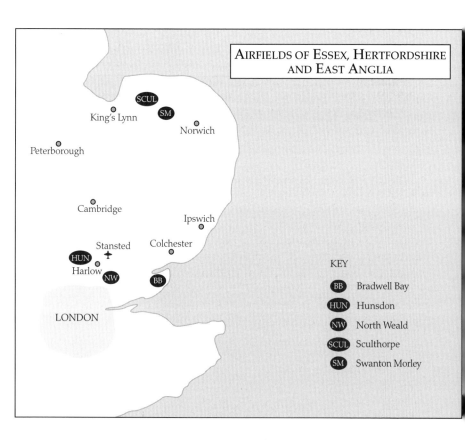

Bradwell Bay

Only used during the Second World War, Bradwell Bay was home to Mosquitos of No. 488 Squadron RNZAF and No. 605 Squadron during the winter of 1943–4 in the period leading up to D-Day. The land has long reverted to agriculture and a memorial now marks the site of the former airfield.

The site of this once busy airfield is located about 20 miles due east of Chelmsford and 5 miles to the north-east of Southminster, on the narrow headland between the estuaries of the Rivers Blackwater and Crouch to the north of Foulness Point. Bradwell Bay was developed during the early part of the Second World War but had been first used as a grass airfield for refuelling and re-arming in the mid-late 1930s by aircraft using the air-to-ground firing ranges at Dengie Flats.

During the Second World War it was initially intended that Bradwell Bay would be used as a satellite airfield for the Hornchurch Sector of Fighter Command but further work was carried out, including the laying of hardened runways and the construction of permanent buildings. This meant that by the time Bradwell Bay opened in April 1942 it was essentially of full airfield status.

For the next year Bradwell Bay was used by a number of squadrons. The airfield's close proximity to the North Sea and Bradwell's three concrete runways meant that it was a welcome sight for many Bomber Command crews returning from operations over Germany when short of fuel or having suffered damage. The airfield was also regularly used by Beaufighters and Mosquitos taking part in intruder or night-fighter operations. No. 29 Squadron moved into Bradwell on 13 May 1943 under the command of Wing Commander Charles Miller. Born in Ireland, Charles Miller had joined the RAF at the outbreak of the Second World War. He initially served in the Middle East with No. 9 Squadron and was awarded the DFC and bar for his gallantry in theatre. He returned to the UK in 1941 and eventually trained as a night-fighter pilot; he joined No. 29 Squadron in August 1942 as a flight commander and scored his first aerial success in a Beaufighter during the night of 26/27 February 1943 when he shot down two Dornier Do17s off Foreness.

In June 1943 control of the airfield was passed to North Weald. A

George Powell-Shedden commanded Bradwell Bay between April and July 1944.

number of fighter squadrons visited Bradwell during the summer of 1943, often when involved in fighter escort operations as Bradwell's location meant that it was a convenient airfield to either refuel or to take off from prior to joining up with bomber formations. In September 1943 No. 29 Squadron left Bradwell for Ford. Arriving in its place was No. 488 Squadron RNZAF from Drem. A month later No. 605 Squadron arrived at Bradwell from Castle Camps and these two squadrons were the mainstays at Bradwell Bay during the latter months of 1943 and early 1944. The Mosquito Xs and XIIs of No. 488 Squadron RNZAF were essentially used for defensive operations whereas the Mosquito VIs of No. 605 Squadron took part in intruder missions across the Channel.

From January 1944 No. 488 Squadron RNZAF was commanded by Wing Commander Richard Haine. Born in Gloucester, Richard Haine had learned to fly whilst still at school before the war and joined the RAF as a sergeant pilot in 1935. In 1940 he was commissioned and posted to No. 600 Squadron, claiming his first success in a Blenheim on 10 May 1940 when he shot down a Bf109 over Rotterdam but was himself forced to make an emergency landing. Having evaded capture, Haine safely returned to the UK. He then flew with a number of squadrons, including spending some time in North Africa, and was awarded the DFC before he took command of No. 488 Squadron RNZAF at Bradwell Bay.

Leading No. 605 Squadron at Bradwell Bay was Wing Commander 'Sammy' Hoare. Having joined the RAF in 1936 Sammy Hoare served initially as a night-fighter pilot with No. 23 Squadron, during which time he scored two kills and claimed a number of aircraft probably destroyed or damaged. By the summer of 1942 he had been given command of the squadron and had converted to the Mosquito; he was also awarded the DSO and the DFC and bar, having by then been credited with six confirmed kills. Hoare was then rested from operations for a year before being given command of No. 605 Squadron in September 1943 immediately prior to moving to Bradwell Bay.

Hoare made an immediate impression and scored his first kill with his new unit on the night of 27/28 September when he shot down a Dornier Do217 near Dedelsdorf. Whilst operating from Bradwell, Sammy Hoare took his personal total to nine after destroying a Junkers Ju188 near Chièvres on the night of 10/11 January 1944 followed by a Messerschmitt Bf109 on the night of 24/25 March. When the squadron left Bradwell Bay on 7 April 1944, Sammy Hoare was promoted to the rank of group captain and was also awarded a bar to his DSO; nonetheless, he continued to fly operational sorties when given the chance. Sadly, having survived the war, Sammy Hoare died in 1947 whilst ferrying a Mosquito to Australia when his aircraft came down on the leg between Singapore and Darwin.

In April 1944 Spitfires of No. 124 Squadron arrived from Church Fenton, Mosquitos of No. 219 Squadron arrived from Colerne and No. 3 Squadron moved north to Ayr for a couple of weeks but soon moved back to Bradwell Bay. By then Bradwell had been numbered No. 150 Airfield and command of the airfield had been passed to Wing Commander George Powell-Shedden. No. 3 Squadron then converted to Tempests but its stay at Bradwell was short lived as at the end of the month No. 150 Airfield moved to Newchurch.

The Mosquitos of No. 219 Squadron remained at Bradwell and carried out intruder patrols over northern France and the Low Countries until August 1944. The Spitfires of No. 124 Squadron also remained at Bradwell and continued to fly bomber escort missions up to and after the D-Day operations. During the air operations of D-Day and after, the Bradwell squadrons were under the command and control of No. 11 Group ADGB.

Bradwell's location close to the North Sea made it an ideal airfield for an air-sea rescue squadron and No. 278 Squadron had also arrived in April. The squadron operated Warwicks and Ansons with its main task to cover the East Anglia area. During its stay at Bradwell, the squadron also operated detachments out of Martlesham Heath during the summer of 1944 and then from Hornchurch during the winter of 1944–5. During the latter months of its stay at Bradwell the squadron converted to the Walrus and extended its area of operation to cover the English Channel.

At the end of August 1944 the Bradwell Bay Wing was formed. No. 124 Squadron had already left Bradwell the previous month and No. 219 Squadron moved to Hunsdon. They were replaced by three Spitfire squadrons that formed the Bradwell Wing; No. 64 and 126 Squadrons arrived from Harrowbeer and No. 611 Squadron from Bolt Head. The wing was in action immediately and on 31 August provided fighter escort for a daytime Bomber Command effort against a number of specific targets in northern France where it was believed V-2 rockets were being built. The wing continued to fly day-fighter escort missions for Bomber Command until the end of the year, although No. 611 Squadron moved to Skeabrae on 3 October, leaving just the two Spitfire squadrons at Bradwell.

The increased number of V-1 attacks being launched against London by Heinkels out at sea saw the arrival of Tempests of No. 501 Squadron on 22 September 1944. The Heinkels were coming into quite close range of London to launch their weapons, typically within about 50 miles of the city, which meant that Bradwell was in a prime location to counter the threat. The Tempest proved a good aircraft for this task but once the V-1 threat had decreased the squadron increasingly became involved in fighter escort missions, the squadron remaining at Bradwell Bay until early March 1945.

During January and February 1945 Bradwell was briefly home to a Czech wing of three Spitfire squadrons but the Spitfires soon moved to Manston, which was a far more forward location to operate from. Before the end of the war Bradwell Bay was used by Mosquitos but once the war in Europe had concluded there was no

**The Mosquito memorial marking the former site of Bradwell
Bay. The nuclear power station is in the background.**

place for Bradwell Bay in the post-war RAF. Flying ceased at the
end of 1945 and the airfield closed in 1946.

The site of the airfield has long reverted to agriculture. It can be
found to the east of Bradwell Waterside and to the south-east of
Bradwell Nuclear Power Station. If you intend to visit the site,
directions will depend on which way you decide to approach the
area. If you are approaching from the north of Chelmsford then get
on to the A12, which bypasses Chelmsford to the east. At Junction
18 take the A414 eastwards through Danbury towards Maldon. Just
before Maldon take the B1018 to Southminster and then the B1021
to Bradwell Waterside. If approaching from the west or south then
from the A127 London to Southend main road, head north along the
A130 towards Chelmsford. After about 3 miles take the A132 to
South Woodham Ferrers, then take the B1012 to Burnham-on-
Crouch and then the B1021 to Bradwell Waterside. As you approach
Bradwell Waterside take the minor road to the east (Trusses Road).
After 600 yards you will come to the road leading to the Nuclear
Power Station. Turn left and you are now at the western end of the
former airfield. The playing field on your left marks the south-west
corner of the main runway, which ran from south-west to north-
east.

The south-west corner of the former airfield at Bradwell Bay. The playing field on the right marks the area where the south-west corner of the main runway once was.

Squadron	Dates at Bradwell Bay	Aircraft Type
29 Squadron	13 May – 3 Sep 43	Mosquito XII
247 Squadron	4 Jun – 10 Jul 43	Typhoon I
198 Squadron	19 – 23 Aug 43	Typhoon I
56 Squadron	23 Aug – 4 Oct 43	Typhoon I
488 Squadron RNZAF	3 Sep 43 – 3 May 44	Mosquito X & XII
605 Squadron	6 Oct 43 – 7 Apr 44	Mosquito VI
3 Squadron	6 Mar – 28 Apr 44	Typhoon I & Tempest V
219 Squadron	1 Apr – 28 Aug 44	Mosquito XVII
124 Squadron	23 Apr – 26 Jul 44	Spitfire VII
278 Squadron	21 Apr – 15 Feb 45	Warwick & Anson
64 Squadron	30 Aug – 28 Dec 44	Spitfire IX
126 Squadron	29 Aug – 30 Dec 44	Spitfire IX
611 Squadron	30 Aug – 3 Oct 44	Spitfire IX
501 Squadron	22 Sep 44 – 3 Mar 45	Tempest V

Hunsdon

This wartime airfield became famous for its part in Operation *Jericho* on 18 February 1944 when Mosquitos of No. 140 Wing, led by Wing Commander 'Pick' Pickard, carried out the famous raid against Amiens Prison where 700 prisoners were being held by the *Gestapo*. The site can still be found today as the memory of this airfield lives on.

In comparison with other airfields in this chapter, the history of Hunsdon is very short. Hunsdon was a wartime airfield only and had no history as an airfield prior to the Second World War and did not survive the peacetime organisation of the RAF.

In 1940 the RAF's increased need for airfields was obvious. Land was identified to the north-west of the town of Harlow and work began to develop the site at the end of the year. The main runway was just over 1,400 yards long and ran from east to west. A second runway of 1,200 yards ran from the south-west to the north-east; both of these runways were later extended. A perimeter track connected the runways and aircraft dispersals.

Crews of No. 487 Squadron pictured at Hunsdon in early 1944.

The airfield opened in February 1941 under the command and control of No. 11 Group. The first unit to operate from Hunsdon was No. 85 Squadron, which arrived from Debden at the beginning of May. During its early days Hunsdon was commanded by the legendary Wing Commander Peter Townsend, although he soon moved on to HQ No. 12 Group. The role of the airfield during 1941–2 was to provide defence for London, particularly at night, and as the war progressed the need for night-fighters around London decreased.

During 1943 the resident units at Hunsdon were Nos 157 and 515 Squadrons. Having arrived at Hunsdon during May 1943, No. 157 Squadron was equipped with Mosquitos and its role included flying patrols over the Bay of Biscay, using Predannack in Cornwall as a forward operating base. As it re-equipped with the Mosquito VI the squadron also conducted bomber escort missions. No. 515 Squadron was equipped with Defiants and Beaufighters. The Defiants were used by the squadron as a trial to fly ahead of bombers with the intention of jamming the enemy radars. However, the Defiants were gradually replaced by Beaufighters, which offered increased range and better survival prospects for the crews. This tactic did not prove particularly successful and No. 515 Squadron was declared non-operational in August, after which the squadron flew calibration sorties for searchlight units. On 8 November No. 410 Squadron RCAF arrived from West Malling; the day after, No. 157 Squadron moved out. The Canadians did not stay at Hunsdon long, although they would later return and spend two further spells at Hunsdon later in the war. No. 515 Squadron also moved out to make way for a new era at Hunsdon.

The formation of 2nd TAF in November 1943 gave the airfield a new lease of life. On 31 December 1943 three Mosquito squadrons arrived at Hunsdon from Sculthorpe: No. 21 Squadron, No. 464 Squadron RAAF and No. 487 Squadron RNZAF. These three Mosquito squadrons operated together as No. 140 Wing. Leading the wing was twenty-eight-year-old Wing Commander 'Pick' Pickard. Born in 1915, Percy Pickard joined the RAF as a pilot in 1937. He flew Wellington bombers with No. 99 Squadron during the Norwegian and French campaigns of 1940. He completed thirty-one operations with the squadron and was awarded the DFC. He was then posted to command No. 311 (Czechoslovak) Squadron, which was the first Czech squadron operating with the RAF. In March

1941 Pickard was awarded the DSO. Pickard went on to serve with No. 9 Squadron and then commanded No. 51 Squadron at Dishforth. During this period he was awarded a bar to his DSO. He then served with No. 161 Squadron and conducted special duties operations between October 1942 and March 1943 for which he was awarded a second bar to his DSO. In October 1943 Pickard was given command of No. 140 Wing.

On 4 January 1944, two of Hunsdon's squadrons took part in a morning raid against a 'Noball' (V-weapon) site at Ruisseauville; one of the Mosquitos from No. 487 Squadron RNZAF was shot down and both crew members were killed. On 6 January Wing Commander Bob Iredale took over command of No. 464 Squadron RAAF. By now the Mosquito squadrons had become quite experienced. Whilst the 'Aussie-Kiwi' mix at Hunsdon seemed to be working well, there were inevitably losses suffered by the

Operation *Jericho*, 18 February 1944. The leader of the raid against the prison at Amiens was Group Captain 'Pick' Pickard. He is seen being helped by his navigator, Flight Lieutenant John Broadley, just before boarding their aircraft at Hunsdon. Sadly, both men were killed on the raid.

squadrons. On 21 January No. 21 Squadron took part in a raid against a 'Noball' site at St Pierre. By now the local defences were well used to the intruders and two of the squadron's Mosquitos were shot down near Bruneval and both aircraft came down in the sea; both crews were killed. There was a further loss for Hunsdon just a week later when a Mosquito of No. 464 Squadron RAAF was shot down near Florennes, Belgium; the crew was killed. Another Mosquito of No. 21 Squadron was lost the following week, on 5 February near Yvetot with the loss of the crew, and the following day another Mosquito of the same squadron was shot down by ground defences during a *Ramrod* operation over Bois Cogerie; again, the crew was killed. Two more Mosquitos were lost on 24 February, one each from Nos 464 and 487 Squadrons, with the loss of both crews. It was, indeed, a difficult period for Hunsford.

Probably the most famous raid carried out by No. 140 Wing was Operation *Jericho*, the raid against Amiens Prison on 18 February 1944 where 700 French prisoners were being held. The majority were members of the French resistance and many were facing certain execution at the hands of the *Gestapo*. The raid was personally approved by the Prime Minister, Winston Churchill, and 2nd TAF was given the task with No. 140 Wing at Hunsdon selected to carry out the raid. Pickard decided to lead the raid himself and the eighteen Mosquitos taking part formed three sections of six, one section from each squadron led by the squadron's commanding officer. The plan was for each section to attack as a wave; the first two were given specific areas to attack with the third wave acting as an airborne reserve should either of the first two waves require support. Each wave was supported by an escort of eight Typhoons, provided by Manston and Westhampnett. Otherwise, the plan was simple; to attack the prison and breach the walls, which would give the prisoners a chance to escape.

During the morning, the eighteen Mosquitos of No. 140 Wing left Hunsdon to attack the prison. 'Pick' Pickard was flying with his long-time navigator and good friend, and also highly decorated, Flight Lieutenant John 'Bill' Broadley DSO DFC DFM of No. 487 Squadron RNZAF. The weather over the southern parts of the UK and North Sea was not good; there was low cloud as well as snow showers, which prevented many of the Manston Typhoons from getting airborne. At Westhampnett, however, the weather was better and the Typhoons all got airborne, although the weather caused further problems when the escort tried to join up with the Mosquitos.

The weather had also hampered the Mosquitos as they flew at low-level across the North Sea. Some had to turn back and eventually fifteen Mosquitos pressed on towards the target. Once at the target, the first two waves of Mosquitos managed to carry out the plan and they successfully breached the two outer walls and destroyed the German guardhouse. As the Mosquitos turned for home they were encountered by Focke-Wulf FW190s but the Typhoons did their job and forced the attackers away. Pickard had remained in the target area throughout the raid, personally directing the operation to the very end. As he turned for home, his Mosquito was attacked by a FW190 and the tail section of his Mosquito was shot away. His aircraft crashed seconds later, killing him and Broadley. The gallant crew are both buried in the St Pierre Cemetery, Amiens.

How successful the Amiens raid was has often been debated over the years. Sadly, just over 100 French prisoners were killed during the raid but more than 250 prisoners managed to escape, although many of these were recaptured. As far as Hunsdon was concerned, the biggest loss was their gallant leader. The AOC No. 2 Group, Air Vice-Marshal Basil Embry, later described Pickard as one who stood out as one of the great airmen of the war and a shining example of British manhood.

No. 140 Wing left Hunsdon on 17 April and moved to Gravesend from where the wing continued its operations during the build-up to the D-Day landings. At the end of April No. 410 Squadron RCAF returned to Hunsdon once more and No. 409 Squadron RCAF moved south from Acklington to join No. 410 Squadron RCAF as a second night-fighter unit at Hunsdon; this unit was also equipped with Mosquito XIIIs. On 28 May a Mosquito crew of No. 410 Squadron RCAF achieved the first air-to-air success over enemy territory using a new version of an AI (air intercept) radar. The Mosquito was equipped with the Mark VIII radar and the crew shot down a Junkers Ju88 over the area of Lille.

During the D-Day operations the squadron provided support over the beachheads and generally around the invasion area. The squadron left Hunsdon on 18 June and was replaced the following day by No. 29 Squadron, which flew intruder missions as well as anti-Diver patrols.

No. 29 Squadron was commanded by Wing Commander George Powell-Shedden from the Isle of Wight. Powell-Shedden was a graduate from the RAF College Cranwell and initially served in the Middle East during the early months of the war. He returned to the UK and flew Hurricanes with No. 242 Squadron during the Battle of Britain. Various postings followed, including command of the RAF stations at Ta Kali in Malta and later Bradwell Bay just before he assumed command of No. 29 Squadron, during which time he was awarded the DFC. In December 1944, George Powell-Shedden handed over command of No. 29 Squadron to Wing Commander John 'Ian' Allan, a Mosquito fighter ace with fourteen confirmed kills. 'Ian' Allan had made his mark over Sicily during the Allied landings in 1943 whilst serving with No. 256 Squadron. Flying with his Australian radar operator, Flight Lieutenant H.I. Davidson, Allan shot down five enemy aircraft in one night bringing his total to ten during the week of the Allied landings alone. The crew were each awarded the DFC and 'Ian' Allan was also awarded the DSO.

No. 29 Squadron would be one of the last units to operate at Hunsdon, finally leaving in February 1945. Other Mosquito squadrons had been and gone, including No. 410 Squadron RCAF,

The Village Hall in Hunsdon. The plaque unveiled by Group Captain John 'Cat's Eyes' Cunningham can be seen on the far left of the building.

which had returned in September 1944 for the last time. At the end of the war the last flying units moved out immediately and Hunsdon closed to flying within days of peace being declared in Europe. The airfield was then placed on care and maintenance and finally closed in July 1947.

After the war the land returned to agriculture and has been owned by various landowners since. Although approval has often been requested for the development of housing, it has so far been refused. Part of the former airfield is currently used by the Hunsdon Microlight Club; the three grass runways used by the club mark the north-eastern part of the former wartime airfield. The last blister hangars were demolished just a few years ago, but parts of the runways and perimeter tracks are still visible.

The local villagers of Hunsdon are undoubtedly proud of the part played by those who served at the airfield during the Second World War. On 8 November 1998 a slate plaque was fixed to the Village Hall by the Parochial Church Council and unveiled by Group Captain John 'Cat's Eyes' Cunningham who had commanded No. 85 Squadron at Hunsdon during the war. On 22

The memorial overlooking the former airfield of Hunsdon. It was erected in May 2005 by the Hunsdon Airfield Group and is a pyramid-shaped plinth mounted by a propeller from a Mosquito.

May 2005 a memorial was also dedicated to the personnel who served at Hunsdon during the Second World War. The memorial is a pyramid-shaped plinth with the top removed to form a flat base on which is mounted the propeller of a Mosquito. The project was the work of the Hunsdon Airfield Group and a service is held by the villagers every year on 18 February to mark the anniversary of the Amiens raid.

Hunsdon is situated to the north-west of Harlow and can be found by taking the A414 westwards from Harlow or eastwards from the A10 London to Ware road. If heading from the A10 take the A414 eastwards. After about one mile cross the A1170 roundabout and continue on the A414 dual carriageway towards Harlow. After about 2 miles, take the B181 north towards the village of Hunsdon. The road then splits with the B181 going left to St Margarets and the B180 right towards Hunsdon. Take the B180 Hunsdon Road for another three miles into the village of Hunsdon. Once at the village centre turn right into Acorn Street. After less than a mile the site of the former airfield can be found on your left. By following the track you will eventually need to bear left to take you to the Microlight Club, which is also the site of the memorial.

One of the former buildings on the western side of the airfield at Hunsdon.

Before leaving the location I suggest you return to Acorn Street and turn right back into the village. After a very short distance you will reach the B180 T-junction. Almost directly opposite you at the junction is the Village Hall, where you can see the plaque unveiled by Group Captain Cunningham in 1998. On your right at the junction is a map showing the layout of Hunsdon, which includes the former airfield.

Squadron	Dates at Hunsdon	Aircraft type
157 Squadron	13 May – 9 Nov 43	Mosquito II & VI
515 Squadron	31 May – 15 Dec 43	Defiant II & Beaufighter II
410 Squadron RCAF	8 Nov – 29 Dec 43	Mosquito II
21 Squadron	31 Dec 43 – 17 Apr 44	Mosquito VI
464 Squadron RAAF	31 Dec 43 – 17 Apr 44	Mosquito VI
487 Squadron RNZAF	31 Dec 43 – 17 Apr 44	Mosquito VI
410 Squadron RCAF	28 Apr – 18 Jun 44	Mosquito XIII
409 Squadron RCAF	30 Apr – 14 May 44	Mosquito XIII
29 Squadron	19 Jun 44 – 22 Feb 45	Mosquito XIII
409 Squadron RCAF	19 Jun – 24 Aug 44	Mosquito XIII
264 Squadron	26 Jul – 11 Aug 44	Mosquito XIII
418 Squadron RCAF	27 Aug – 21 Nov 44	Mosquito VI
410 Squadron RCAF	9 – 22 Sep 44	Mosquito XXX
219 Squadron	28 Aug – 10 Oct 44	Mosquito XVII & XXX

North Weald

The origins of this famous airfield date back to the First World War. Following the formation of 2nd TAF North Weald was designated No. 132 Airfield as part of No. 84 Group and was home to Spitfire IXs of No. 19 Wing and then No. 132 (Norwegian) Wing. North Weald was later home to jet fighter squadrons of the post-war RAF and the site is still used today for a wide range of activities.

One of the RAF's most famous wartime airfields, North Weald still exists today and is located about 3 miles to the south-east of Harlow in Essex; the airfield can be clearly seen when driving along the M11, to the eastern side of the motorway just to the south of Junction 7. The origins of this airfield date back to the First World War when land was developed to the west of North Weald Bassett. The first aircraft to operate from the airfield were a detachment BE2Cs of No. 39 Squadron in the home defence of London.

After the First World War the airfield initially remained empty until it was developed during the late 1920s as a fighter airfield.

Spitfire IX of No. 332 Squadron, one of two Norwegian squadrons at North Weald during early 1944.

New hangars and buildings were erected and other facilities improved. Towards the end of 1927 Siskins of No. 56 Squadron moved in and North Weald was operational once more. As part of the RAF's expansion programme during the mid-1930s, more squadrons arrived at North Weald and the airfield was transformed into one of the most advanced fighter airfields in Fighter Command. The northern boundary was initially extended to accommodate four grass runways but by the beginning of the Second World War there were two hard runways. The main runway was essentially a north–south direction and the second runway crossing more towards east–west. An asphalt perimeter track was also laid to ease movement around the western side of the airfield. Aircraft were accommodated in two A-type hangars and four blister hangars, with an additional four 'extra over' blister hangars. Extensive airfield lighting meant that night operations were available. North Weald also had the use of nearby Stapleford Tawney as a satellite airfield and also had a decoy airfield at Nazeing.

North Weald was extensively used throughout the Battle of Britain by Hurricanes of No. 11 Group. When the battle opened North Weald was home to Nos 56 and 151 Squadrons. Because of North Weald's location just to the north of London it was quite normal during the early stages of the battle for the Hurricanes to deploy further south to Manston at first light and then return to North Weald at the end of the day. The two resident squadrons were replaced by Nos 249 and 257 Squadrons in August and Blenheims of No. 25 Squadron also moved into North Weald at the beginning of September. North Weald understandably became one of the *Luftwaffe*'s priority targets during August and September, and this resulted in many of the station's assets having to re-locate in the local area. When the *Luftwaffe* turned its attention away from Fighter Command's airfields and on to the city of London, it provided a welcome break for North Weald's personnel.

Many famous fighter pilots flew from North Weald during the Battle of Britain. The station was led by Wing Commander Victor Beamish who flew with the squadrons whenever the opportunity presented itself. He was awarded both the DSO and the DFC for his outstanding leadership during the battle and he became a legend at North Weald. Another of the airfield's legends was Squadron Leader Bob Tuck who commanded No. 257 Squadron at North

Weald. Tuck went on to become one of the RAF's highest-scoring aces with twenty-seven confirmed kills for which he was awarded the DSO, and two bars to his DFC.

North Weald remained a front-line fighter airfield during the period immediately after the Battle of Britain and many fighter squadrons served from the airfield during the next couple of years. During 1942 the squadrons based at North Weald were Spitfire V units with the Norwegian squadrons Nos 331 and 332 Squadrons amongst the regular visitors; in fact, with the exception of a week here and a week there, No. 331 Squadron would have a permanent presence at North Weald until the end of March 1944. In March 1943 No. 124 Squadron arrived from Duxford having just taken delivery of Spitire Mk VIIs, which gave the squadron the capability to operate at high altitude. During the next four months the squadron operated a detachment of aircraft in the south-west of the country where it flew a mix of high altitude interceptions and convoy patrols.

North Weald received its first Mustangs during November 1943. The first Mustang squadron to arrive was No. 4 Squadron from Odiham. But the squadron only remained at North Weald for two weeks before it moved on to Sawbridgeworth from where two more Mustang squadrons moved to North Weald – Nos 63 and 168 Squadrons, which both operated mainly in the low-level tactical reconnaissance role.

On 12 December No. 168 Squadron lost one of its pilots when two of its Mustangs collided in mid-air. North Weald suffered a further loss just two days later when a Mustang of No. 63 Squadron was shot down over Cassel.

Commanding No. 132 (Norwegian) Wing during this period was the Dane Lieutenant-Colonel Kaj Birksted. Having fled Norway for England in 1940, Birksted had scored his first successes of the war whilst serving with No. 331 Squadron during 1942. He commanded the squadron between September 1942 and April 1943 when he was given command of No. 132 (Norwegian) Wing. On 20 December, whilst leading the wing over Northern France, he shot down a Focke-Wulf FW190 over Cambrai – his ninth confirmed kill of the war. During the same action his wing colleagues shot down a further two FW190s. On 3 January 1944 two of No. 331 Squadron's Spitfires collided over North Weald with the loss of one pilot killed. The surviving pilot was the Norwegian Captain Bjorn Björnstad who was one of the squadron's leading scorers having already been confirmed with five kills.

No. 63 Squadron left North Weald in January 1944 and was replaced by two more Mustang units, Nos 2 and 268 Squadrons. On 22 January No. 268 Squadron resumed operations having returned south after a break in Scotland. The following day North Weald's Mustangs escorted Marauders during a *Ramrod* mission during the afternoon without incident, although one enemy Focke-Wulf FW190 was claimed as damaged. However, the Norwegian pilots were far busier during the afternoon and shot down three FW190s over Breteuil. One was shot down by Lieutenant-Colonel Kaj Birksted, his tenth of the war, and another was shot down by Major Werner Christie who was commanding officer of No. 332 Squadron; this was Christie's fifth success of the war.

During the afternoon of 11 February, Lieutenant Fredrik Fearnley was part of a formation from No. 331 Squadron over northern France when he came across Focke-Fulf FW190s between Dieppe and Lille. The experienced Fearnley had served with the squadron since early 1942 and was well used to air-to-air combat with Focke-Wulf FW190s having personally destroyed four of the type in October 1943 alone. During the following combat Fearnley brought his total of FW190s destroyed to five when he shot down one to the south-west of Lille. Sadly, however, this gallant Norwegian would not survive much longer. Two weeks later he was killed when he was shot down by ground defences during a low-level strafing attack against St Trond airfield. The following month it was announced that Fredrik Fearnley had been awarded the DFC.

More changes followed and the Mustangs were replaced by Spitfire IXs during February and March. As the Allied invasion was now drawing nearer, the squadrons based furthest from the Channel were moved to bases along the south coast. Therefore, on 31 March, No. 132 Airfield moved from North Weald to Bognor and by the end of May no fewer than six Spitfire squadrons had arrived and left North Weald.

As its location was too far north, North Weald was not used for operations over the invasion area during the D-Day period. The squadrons that had passed through had been moved further south to increase their range and endurance over the Channel and the Normandy beaches. Instead, North Weald was home to two very different types of squadron during the summer of 1944. No. 116

Squadron was a calibration squadron and was equipped with a mix of aircraft, namely Tiger Moths, Oxfords and Hurricanes. The second squadron was No. 287 Squadron, which was used in a variety of roles such as target-towing and for gun-laying exercises; this squadron was also equipped with Oxfords as well as Martinets. The squadrons remained until the end of August when North Weald was once again home to a number of different squadrons until the end of the war.

At the end of the war the airfield was transferred to Transport Command and for a while there was little flying activity from North Weald. In 1949 command and control was passed back to Fighter Command and the airfield prepared itself for the RAF's new generation of jet fighters. For the next ten years life at North Weald was busy until the airfield was placed on care and maintenance in 1958 and the RAF moved out all together in 1964. North Weald was then handed over to the Army in 1966, although it did remain open for light aircraft flying. In 1969 the airfield was appropriately used during the making of the film *Battle of Britain*. During the 1970s a

The airfield museum marks the position of the former main entrance to North Weald. The permanent memorial is dedicated to those who served at the airfield.

number of air shows took place from the airfield, including the first International Air Tattoo in 1971, and from the mid-1980s North Weald became host to the world famous Fighter Meet.

North Weald continues to be home to a wide range of different aircraft and activities and there are several old buildings still in existence. The memory of its former days lives on with the North Weald Airfield Museum, which is located in the former station office adjacent to what used to be the main entrance to the airfield. The museum is on Hurricane Way in North Weald and it can be found to the north-east of Epping on the B181 Epping to Ongar road. Access is via the village of North Weald and not via the present day entrance to the main airfield. The address of the museum is: Ad Astra House, 6 Hurricane Way, North Weald, Essex CM16 6AA. It is open every weekend and most bank holidays from Easter to October from midday to 5.00 p.m. Admission is £1.50 for adults and £1 for seniors and children under sixteen years old. Group visits are welcome at other times but by prior arrangement only. The museum is a charitable trust and depends on income from entry, membership and donations. More details about the history of North Weald can be obtained from the North Weald Airfield Museum website (www.northwealdairfield.org).

In 2000 a permanent memorial located next to the museum was dedicated to those who served at North Weald. Access to the airfield is restricted but group tours can be arranged with sufficient notice and subject to the Airfield Manager's agreement. The airfield can easily be found on the B181 Epping to Ongar road, to the north-east of Epping and to the south-east of Junction 7 of the M11.

Squadron	Dates at North Weald	Aircraft Type
331 Squadron	4 May 42 – 31 Mar 44	Spitfire V & IX
332 Squadron	19 Jun 42 – 31 Mar 44	Spitfire V & IX
124 Squadron	12 Mar – 26 Jul 43	Spitfire VII
4 Squadron	15 – 30 Nov 43	Mustang I
63 Squadron	30 Nov 43 – 21 Jan 44	Mustang I
168 Squadron	30 Nov 43 – 6 Mar 44	Mustang I
268 Squadron	17 Jan – 1 Mar 44	Mustang I
2 Squadron	22 Jan – 29 Feb 44	Mustang I

66 Squadron	1 – 31 Mar 44	Spitfire IX
1 Squadron	3 – 22 Apr 44	Spitfire IX
127 Squadron	23 Apr – 17 May 44	Spitfire IX
33 Squadron	27 Apr – 17 May 44	Spitfire IX
74 Squadron	24 Apr – 17 May 44	Spitfire IX
116 Squadron	2 Jul – 27 Aug 44	Hurricane/Tiger Moth/Oxford
287 Squadron	4 Jul – 27 Aug 44	Oxford/Martinet

Sculthorpe

Opened in 1943 Sculthorpe was designated No. 140 Airfield as part of No. 2 Group and was home to three squadrons of Mosquito VIs during the early days of 2nd TAF. The airfield was later used by American bombers of Strategic Air Command.

Located about 12 miles to the north-east of King's Lynn in Norfolk, just to the west of the small town of Fakenham, is the village of Sculthorpe. The former airfield at Sculthorpe was first developed as a satellite for West Raynham during 1942 and opened as RAF Sculthorpe in January 1943 within the organisation of No. 2 Group, Bomber Command. The first resident squadron was No. 342 'Free French' Squadron, equipped with Bostons, which moved in on 15 May 1943 and remained at Sculthorpe until July.

When the Bostons moved out, the first Mosquitos of No. 464 Squadron RAAF and No. 487 Squadron RNZAF arrived from Methwold. These two squadrons were joined by No. 21 Squadron in September and the wing worked up together to operate in the fighter-bomber role, both by day and by night. These three squadrons became No. 140 Airfield and in October Wing Commander 'Pick' Pickard was given command of the wing; Pickard would later lead the wing from Hunsdon during the famous Mosquito raid against Amiens Prison in February 1944.

During the last months of 1943 Sculthorpe's Mosquito wing carried out numerous attacks against selected targets in France;

these targets included Germany's flying bomb sites. During mid-November, No. 464 Squadron sent detachments to Bradwell Bay and Ford for two weeks to start its training for its night-intruder role; something the squadron would be asked to undertake during the next period of its operations.

On 4 December No. 487 Squadron RNZAF lost one of its Mosquitos during an afternoon raid against Borkum; the crew was killed. The squadron was now becoming increasingly involved in operational sorties across occupied Europe, in particular against rail targets, transportation routes and V-weapon sites. This was, however, to be a costly period for the squadron. In addition to the crew lost on 4 December, the squadron lost two more aircraft on 10 December with both crews killed. On 22 December the Mosquitos of No. 21 Squadron took part in the largest operation by No. 2 Group against 'Noball' sites. The total group effort involved thirty-six Bostons from Hartfordbridge, twenty-four Mitchells from

An armourer servicing a Mosquito. Sculthorpe was home to three Mosquito squadrons at the end of 1943, which carried out numerous attacks against selected targets in France.

Many of Sculthorpe's former domestic buildings are now used as part of Tattersett Business Park, although many lie empty and somewhat derelict.

Dunsfold and eleven Mosquitos from No. 21 Squadron. Later in the day, twenty-six Mosquitos from all three Sculthorpe squadrons took part in a further raid against St Agathe. It was a successful day for the squadrons.

On the last day of the year the wing moved to Hunsdon. Control of Sculthorpe then passed to No. 100 Group and B-17 Fortresses of No. 214 Squadron moved in from Downham Market. In May 1944 the squadron moved out and the airfield closed for major redevelopment work; the future of the airfield was for the operation of heavy bombers.

Sculthorpe was closed for more than four years and did not re-open until the end of 1948. The airfield was then used by heavy bombers of America's Strategic Air Command during the late 1940s and early 1950s; Sculthorpe's extended runways making it an ideal operating base. Units of the US Air Force continued to operate from Sculthorpe until 1962.

The airfield is to the west of Sculthorpe village, on the northern side of the A148 towards King's Lynn where the road meets the B1454. Although there is no access to the site, the best view of the

The view across the airfield of Sculthorpe from Tattersett Business Park. Hangars as well as the former air traffic control tower can clearly be seen.

airfield can be found by turning right off the A148 along the B1454 towards Syderstone. After about one mile, take the first turning right into Sculthorpe Boulevard. This narrow road takes you down to the part of the former domestic site where a number of buildings are currently used as part of the Tattersett Business Park. It is easy to park the car and get a good view of the airfield, air traffic control tower and hangars.

Squadron	Dates at Sculthorpe	Aircraft
No. 342 'Free French' Squadron	15 May – 19 Jul 43	Boston III
No. 464 Squadron RAAF	21 Jul – 31 Dec 43	Mosquito VI
No. 487 Squadron RNZAF	20 Jul – 31 Dec 43	Mosquito VI
No. 21 Squadron	27 Sep – 31 Dec 43	Mosquito VI
No. 214 Squadron	16 Jan – 16 May 44	B-17 Fortress II

Swanton Morley

When 2nd TAF formed in November 1943 this airfield was home to Mitchell II bombers of No. 226 Squadron as part of No. 2 Group. Swanton Morley remained an RAF station until 1995 and is now used by the Army.

Just 3 miles to the north-east of Dereham in Norfolk is the village of Swanton Morley. Overlooking the Wensum Valley, Swanton Morley was another airfield that came into existence as a result of the Second World War, although, unlike some other airfields in Norfolk, Swanton Morley was identified as a suitable site before the war commenced. The grass airfield was not ready to open until the late summer of 1940. A Type J hangar had been erected on the technical site and a number of hard standings had been constructed around the airfield.

The first unit to arrive at Swanton Morley was No. 105 Squadron, equipped with Blenheims, which moved into the new airfield from Watton at the end of October 1940. Swanton Morley was under the command and control of No. 2 Group, Bomber Command.

The long-term resident unit at Swanton Morley during 1942–3 was No. 226 Squadron, which moved in during December 1941 and stayed until February 1944. During this time the squadron initially operated Bostons and then converted to Mitchells in May 1943, to carry out daylight attacks against enemy ports and shipping across the North Sea. The squadron had been joined at the end of March by Bostons of No. 88 Squadron, which operated at Swanton Morley until August when it moved to Hartford Bridge. Two weeks later, Mitchells of No. 305 'Weilkopolski' Squadron arrived at Swanton Morley, although this unit would only remain for two months before moving on to Lasham during November.

The airfield facilities were improved during 1942–3. Four T2 hangars were erected, more hard standings were constructed around the airfield and an airfield perimeter track was laid. There had also been work carried out on the technical and domestic sites, which had increased the capacity of the station. Following the formation of 2nd TAF in November 1943, Swanton Morley was not given an official airfield number. This was unlike other airfields within 2nd TAF because No. 226 Squadron was to essentially operate alone from the airfield. However, the formation of 2nd TAF

Swanton Morley, April 1944. Ground crew preparing Mosquitos of No. 464 Squadron for another mission.

did see a change in tactics for No. 226 Squadron as it then started to carry out daylight raids on enemy communications targets and enemy airfields across the Channel.

On 25 November the Mitchells of No. 226 Squadron took part in an important raid against the HQ of the German's Todt Organization (a Third *Reich* civil and military engineering group) located in the village of Audinghen in northern France. The Mitchells were joined in the attack by Bostons from Hartfordbridge. The German defences around the location of the HQ were understandably very strong and many of the squadron's Mitchells were hit by anti-aircraft fire but only one aircraft was lost; the crew were all killed when the aircraft crashed near Dover trying to make it home.

On 23 December No. 226 Squadron joined forces with Mitchells of No. 320 Squadron from Dunsfold to attack Puchervin; all the squadron's Mitchells returned to Swanton Morley safely. At the end of the year, Typhoons of No. 3 Squadron arrived from Manston under the command of Squadron Leader Allan Dredge. The Typhoons took part in low-level and dive-bombing attacks against selected targets in northern France until February 1944 when the squadron returned to Manston. At the same time, No. 226 Squadron left Swanton Morley for Hartfordbridge and from there it would eventually move across to mainland Europe where it would continue operations until the end of the war.

A month passed before Mosquitos of No. 464 Squadron RAAF arrived from Hunsdon to carry out training exercises with the Army, followed by Mitchell bombers of No. 98 Squadron from Dunsfold. However, these two units only stayed at Swanton Morley for two weeks before they returned to their former units. The squadrons were replaced by two more Mosquito units: No. 613 Squadron from Lasham and No. 487 Squadron RNZAF from Gravesend, although, again, these two squadrons also only stayed at Swanton Morley for a matter of days before returning to their former units. Whilst at Swanton Morley, the Mosquito squadrons were involved in many fighter-bomber low-level precision attacks as well as night intruder missions. One example was on 11 April when Mosquitos of No. 613 Squadron took part in a special operation by No. 2 Group against a building in The Hague,

Following the Worthing Road from the main entrance to Robertson Barracks tracks part of the perimeter of the former airfield at Swanton Morley but this gate provides just about the only vantage point.

Holland, where the Germans held their records and documents relating to Dutch resistance fighters. The raid was a success with no losses to the squadron.

By the end of April both No. 613 Squadron and No. 487 Squadron RNZAF had left Swanton Morley and the airfield played no major part in the final preparations for D-Day. At the end of 1944 control of the airfield was passed to No. 100 Group. With the demise of No. 100 Group after the war, little use was made of Swanton Morley until the end of 1946 when No. 4 Radio School moved in. The school was later re-named No. 1 Air Signallers' School and the Air Electronic School. The school remained at Swanton Morley until 1957.

Swanton Morley was then used for gliding and by RAF ground units until its closure in September 1995. The airfield was then taken over by the Army as Robertson Barracks in 1996 and is now home to the Light Dragoons. The airfield can be found by taking the A47 eastwards from Dereham and then the B1147 to Swanton Morley. The airfield is to the north-west of the village of Swanton Morley,

Graves of RAF airmen lie in the village church at Swanton Morley.

towards the village of Worthing, and can be found by taking
Mann's Lane from Swanton Morley. Then turn left into Hoe Road
East and then right into Hoe Road North. Without going into
Robertson Barracks, which has to be by appointment only, there is
little to see of the former airfield from the narrow country lanes and
overgrown hedgerows that surround the site of the barracks.
Following Worthing Road from the barracks the road takes you
around the outer perimeter of the former airfield but there really is
little, if anything, to see.

Squadron	Dates at Swanton Morley	Aircraft Type
No. 226 Squadron	9 Dec 41 – 13 Feb 44	Boston III & Mitchell II
No. 88 Squadron	30 Mar – 19 Aug 43	Boston III
No. 305 'Weilkopolski' Squadron	5 Sep – 18 Nov 43	Mitchell II
No. 3 Squadron	28 Dec 43 – 14 Feb 44	Typhoon I
No. 464 Squadron RAAF	25 Mar – 8 Apr 44	Mosquito VI
No. 98 Squadron	27 Mar – 10 Apr 44	Mitchell II
No. 613 Squadron	11 – 24 Apr 44	Mosquito VI
No. 487 Squadron RNZAF	25 – 30 Apr 44	Mosquito VI

CHAPTER 4

Airfields of Greater London

The area around London has understandably been at the forefront of aviation in this country. The combination of the birth of aviation and the First World War meant that many airfields appeared close to the capital for a variety of reasons. As far as military aviation is concerned airfields around London were first used during the First World War by Home Defence squadrons of the Royal Flying Corps to deter attacks on the capital by German bombers and Zeppelin airships. Then again during the 1930s the RAF's Expansion Scheme saw the appearance of a number of new airfields as well as the resurrection of others. Many of these were pivotal in Fighter Command's success during the Battle of Britain. In between the two world wars the rapid expansion of commercial aviation saw the need for yet more airfields as civilian companies and airlines contested the market share of an industry that saw the enormous potential for air passengers and commercial freight.

Depending on where boundaries are drawn, there are more than fifty airfields in and around Greater London. For this chapter I have used the M25 as the outer perimeter and have included the six airfields within the M25 that played a vital part in 2nd TAF's build up and contribution to the Allied invasion of Europe. Most of these airfields need little or no introduction. Names such as Biggin Hill, Hornchurch and Kenley have all written their own chapters in the RAF's history whereas Fairlop and Heston are less known. The sixth airfield, Northolt, is the only one that has survived the post-war era and is still very much a fully active RAF station today.

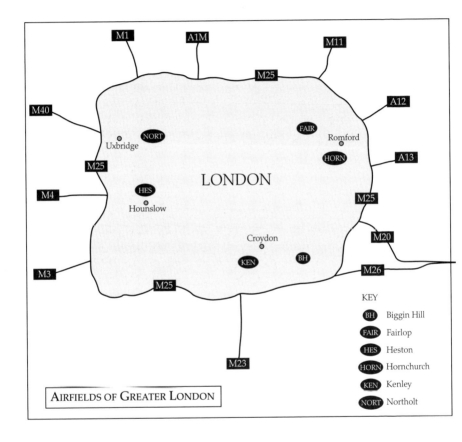

AIRFIELDS OF GREATER LONDON

Biggin Hill

One of the most famous RAF airfields, the origins of Biggin Hill date back to the First World War. Following the formation of 2nd TAF, Biggin Hill was designated No. 126 Airfield of No. 83 Group and was home to three Canadian squadrons of Spitfires of No. 17 Wing during the winter of 1943–4. The site was used by the RAF until 1992 and is now Biggin Hill Airport.

Ask anyone today to name a famous fighter airfield of the Second World War and Biggin Hill would surely be amongst the most common of answers. Like many of the RAF's famous airfields, Biggin Hill dates back to the First World War but the airfield is legendary and it has rightly remained as a symbol of RAF history until today.

Until the mid-nineteenth century the area was known as Aperfield Manor, which consisted of farms and cottages within the parish of Cudham. By the early 1900s Biggin Hill, named after Biggin Hill Farm, was a small settlement of just 500 people. By 1914 most of the Aperfield estate had been sold for development, although the Cudham Lodge estate was still traditionally farmed. As the First World War moved into its third year, the expansion of the Royal Flying Corps meant that sites were needed for aircraft and for testing communications equipment. The area of Cudham Lodge was considered ideal as it was on reasonably high ground, flat and fog-free. By February 1917 the site was being used for communications testing but the introduction by the Germans of long-range bombing missions against London meant that aircraft were moved from airfields north of the city to the south for the protection of London.

The first resident unit was No. 141 Squadron, which arrived in February 1918 as a home defence squadron for the protection of London, and was equipped with the Bristol F2b. The squadron scored its only victory of the war whilst operating from Biggin Hill when a Gotha bomber was shot down on the night of 19/20 May 1918.

Whilst several of the RAF's airfields had no future in post-war Britain, Biggin Hill remained a front-line station for the RAF. Sopwith Snipes of No. 56 Squadron moved in from Hawkinge in May 1923 to become part of the RAF's small post-war fighter force.

The squadron was initially involved in service trials of new aircraft such as the Hawker Woodcock and Hawker Hedgehog before it took delivery of the Gloster Grebe in September 1924. For the next three years No. 56 Squadron operated from Biggin Hill before it moved to North Weald at the end of 1927 so that development work on the airfield could begin.

There then followed five years of major work on the airfield, which saw the construction of new hangars, technical and administrative buildings, and domestic accommodation. By the end of the summer of 1932 work had been completed and Biggin Hill was once again an active airfield.

The first units to operate from the new airfield were No. 23 Squadron and No. 32 Squadron equipped with Bristol Bulldogs, which both arrived from Kenley in September 1932. Both squadrons served together at Biggin until No. 23 Squadron moved out at the end of 1936. By the opening period of the Second World War, Biggin was home to two squadrons of Hurricanes, Nos 32 and 79 Squadrons, and No. 601 Squadron equipped with Blenheims. During the Battle of France the Hurricanes of No. 79 Squadron moved across the Channel whilst No. 32 Squadron spent much time operating out of Gravesend and Manston in support of the air battle over France.

Construction work at Biggin, which included the hardening of the main runway to 1,600 yards long, was completed by the opening phase of the Battle of Britain and the airfield was one of No. 11 Group's and Fighter Command's most vital stations. It was a Sector Airfield and, together with Kenley, protected the approaches to London from the south and south-east. During the Battle of Britain seven squadrons operated from Biggin: Nos 32 and 79 Squadrons (Hurricanes), Nos 610, 72, 92 and 74 Squadrons (Spitfires) and No. 141 Squadron (Defiants). The amount of air activity peaked during August 1940 when there were over 100 sorties per day flown.

Biggin was attacked for the first time on 18 August. It was just after 1.30 p.m. when the attack took place and the raid lasted just over an hour. Fortunately, most of the bombs fell on the nearby golf course but the airfield was left cratered and there was damage to the main runway. This attack was to be the first of many as during the following two weeks there were attacks almost daily as Biggin became a major target for the *Luftwaffe*. One of the heaviest days of attacks was on Friday 30 August when Biggin was very nearly knocked out of the battle. The first raid took place at midday from medium-level and the second from low-level at 6.00 p.m. It was the latter by Ju88s that caused the most damage. There was little notice and the station personnel hardly had the time to take cover. The attack proved to be devastating with several buildings destroyed, including a hangar, and severe damage to many more. The gas and electricity supplies had been cut and casualties were high; thirty-nine station personnel were killed and more than twenty wounded. The airfield had lost all communications and command and control of the sector's assets was temporarily passed to Hornchurch; this was at a time when Hornchurch was also controlling the airfields of Rochford, Gravesend and Redhill.

The temporary loss of Biggin Hill was a significant blow to No. 11 Group. Repair work was hampered the following morning as there were warnings of further attacks; indeed, there were two further attacks in the afternoon. There was another heavy attack during the following day bringing the number to five in just forty-eight hours. Biggin Hill had become one of the two most bombed airfields of Fighter Command during the Battle of Britain; the other was Hornchurch. The contribution of the squadrons and personnel at Biggin Hill during the Battle of Britain ensured that the airfield would take its place in history. After the battle, Fighter Command turned to offensive operations. Several different fighter squadrons operated from Biggin during 1941 and 1942, during which time the Spitfires had been joined by Typhoons.

In May 1943 the station scored its thousandth victory, which was a record for any station during the Second World War, and in September the St George's Chapel of Remembrance was dedicated.

The Station Commander at Biggin Hill during this period was the legendary Group Captain 'Sailor' Malan, who had assumed command on 1 January 1943. Born in South Africa in 1910, Malan had joined the RAF in 1935. His first squadron was No. 74 Squadron and he had claimed his first victory in the skies over Dunkirk during the heavy aerial fighting in May 1940. By the time he had been promoted to the rank of group captain, Malan had been credited with at least twenty-seven aircraft destroyed for which he had been awarded the DSO and bar and the DFC and bar. No stranger to Biggin Hill, Malan had risen through the ranks with No. 74 Squadron and had commanded the squadron at Biggin Hill during the Battle of Britain.

When 2nd TAF formed in November 1943, 'Sailor' Malan handed over command of Biggin Hill to Group Captain Hugh Maxwell to take up his new appointment in command of No. 19 Wing within the new 2nd TAF command structure. At the time he took up his appointment, Maxwell, a former Army officer, was thirty-four years old. He had commanded No. 600 Squadron at Catterick during the Battle of Britain, for which he was awarded the DSO, and had served at No. 13 Group before being appointed as the Station Commander of Hornchurch in July 1943. Having taken up his new appointment at Biggin Hill, Hugh Maxwell would remain its commanding officer until the end of the war.

Biggin Hill was designated No. 126 Airfield under the organisation of No. 83 Group and was home to three Canadian squadrons of Spitfire IXs, all of which had arrived from Staplehurst in Kent during October 1943. The first squadron to arrive was No. 401 Squadron, commanded by Squadron Leader E.L. Neal DFC, on 12 October, followed the next day by Nos 411 and 412 Squadrons, commanded by Squadron Leader I. Ormston DFC and Squadron Leader George Keefer DFC respectively.

No. 401 'Ram' Squadron was previously No. 1 Squadron RCAF and had first arrived in England in June 1940. It had seen action during the Battle of Britain and was renumbered No. 401 Squadron in May 1941 to avoid confusion with the RAF's own No. 1 Squadron. This was to be the squadron's third and final tour of duty at Biggin Hill, having previously operated from the airfield between October 1941 to March 1942 and briefly during August to September of the same year. No. 411 'Grizzly Bear' and No. 412 'Falcon' Squadrons had both formed in June 1941 and this was both squadrons' first time of operating from Biggin.

When the young Canadian George Keefer led No. 412 Squadron into Biggin Hill on 13 October he was still just twenty-two years old but was already a veteran of air combat and had earned his DFC a year before whilst operating in the Middle East. Born in New York to Canadian parents, Keefer had joined the RCAF in October 1940 at the age of nineteen. Having completed pilot training Keefer was posted to No. 274 Squadron in the Middle East where he flew Hurricanes over the Western Desert. Keefer had scored his first kill on 7 December 1941 and added three more to his total during the next six months. By spring 1942 his squadron's Hurricanes had been modified for ground-attack duties during the Battle of El

At just twenty years old, the young Canadian George Keefer led No. 412 Squadron RCAF at Biggin Hill during October 1943. He was eventually credited with at least twelve enemy aircraft destroyed and finished the war with a DSO and bar and the DFC and bar.

Alamein and the squadron began moving forward through Libya as the 8th Army captured a number of enemy airfields. Keefer then carried out instructor duties in the Middle East before he returned to the UK in May 1943 and took command of No. 412 Squadron at Friston the following month. Since taking command just four months earlier, the squadron had moved to Redhill and Staplehurst, spending only a few weeks at each, before making its more 'permanent' move to Biggin Hill.

Although the formation of 2nd TAF had seen a change in structure of the RAF, the three Canadian squadrons spent much of their time operating in the same way as previously, such as operating across the Channel on *Rodeo* and *Ramrod* operations and taking part in several training exercises. With the Allied invasion of mainland Europe getting closer the number of exercises increased, in particular those involving the Army and Navy.

A Spitfire of No. 401 Squadron RCAF at Biggin Hill with a flypast taking part in the background.

On 23 November No. 411 Squadron RCAF lost one of its Spitfires over the Channel; the pilot was killed. This was the same day that Nos 401 and 412 Squadrons flew their first operations with their new Spitfire IXs. Three days later, twenty-three-year-old Canadian pilot Flight Lieutenant Jack Sheppard of No. 401 Squadron claimed the squadron's first kill with the new type when he shot down a Focke-Wulf FW190 over Achiet airfield; this was Sheppard's first success, although he would go on to achieve four more kills during the next eight months for which he would be awarded the DFC.

On 29 November all three squadrons were involved in providing fighter escort for more than seventy B-26 Marauders, which were detailed to attack the Belgian airfield at Chièvres. The formation was bounced by Focke-Wulf FW190s and during the following combat the Spitfires successfully beat off the attackers. Flying Officer Lorne Cameron of No. 401 Squadron was credited with shooting down one of the FW190s over the target, his second confirmed kill. Unfortunately, however, No. 412 Squadron lost one of its pilots. Two days later No. 411 Squadron RCAF was also escorting B-26s when the squadron had mixed fortunes; two

The Canadian Lorne Cameron joined No. 401 Squadron RCAF at Biggin Hill in November 1943. He became a flight commander the following month and was then given command of the squadron in January 1944. He was awarded the DFC in April 1944 for his gallantry whilst leading the squadron.

FW190s were shot down but so too were two of the squadron's Spitfires; one pilot was killed.

Two of the three squadrons saw a change in command in December. Command of No. 411 Squadron was handed to Squadron Leader J.D. McFarlane and command of No. 401 Squadron was handed over to Squadron Leader Lorne Cameron. Born in 1922 and brought up in Manitoba, Canada, Cameron had joined the RCAF in January 1941. He had claimed his first victory on his twenty-first birthday whilst serving with No. 402 Squadron and was posted to No. 401 Squadron as a flight commander at Biggin Hill in November 1943. Whilst operating with the squadron over Chièvres airfield on 29 November he destroyed a FW190, his second confirmed kill, and added a third on 20 December, a Ju88 over Brussels, just a few days after taking command of the squadron.

On 30 December, one of Canada's most famous fighter pilots scored his thirty-first and final kill of the war whilst serving with No. 412 Squadron at Biggin Hill. Flight Lieutenant George 'Screwball' Beurling had only just joined the squadron but he was already a national hero. The son of a Swedish father and English mother, Beurling was born in Montreal, Canada, in 1921. Although he lacked the educational qualifications to join the RCAF, he had learnt to fly privately but was too young to be granted a licence. Beurling first attempted to join the Finnish Air Force during the Russo–Finnish war and then the RAF during the Battle of Britain. On both occasions he was turned away; he was too young to join the Finnish Air Force and then failed to produce his birth certificate when trying to join the RAF. However, after making the round-trip back to Canada he eventually joined the RAF as a sergeant pilot in September 1940.

'Screwball' Beurling made his name during the air battle for Malta. Twenty-seven of his kills were achieved whilst flying Spitfire Vs with No. 249 Squadron during the summer of 1942; fifteen of these kills came during July alone. Beurling was considered by some to be a somewhat different character to other fighter pilots at the time. He did not drink or smoke and his only bad word was generally 'screwball'; hence his nickname. He was also often happier when fighting alone and he was happy being a non-commissioned pilot. His opposition to disciplined tactics earlier in the war had made him unpopular with his superiors; hence his posting to Malta. However, he was considered a master of aerial combat and studied air-to-air gunnery to the finest degree. Having achieved his seventeenth kill he was awarded a bar to his DFM. Beurling's refusal to be commissioned was eventually over-turned and he was effectively ordered to take a commission in August 1942. By the end of October he had scored twenty-nine victories and had added a DSO and DFC to his awards.

Having been rested from operations, Beurling was then sent home to Canada for a publicity tour. He returned to the UK in the summer of 1943 and was briefly an instructor before transferring to the RCAF. Whilst serving with No. 403 Squadron he added a further victory to his total. Having then initially been posted to No. 126 Wing Headquarters, Beurling was posted to No. 412 Squadron at Biggin Hill at the end of November, just days before his twenty-second birthday. Beurling's thirty-first kill, on 30 December 1943, was a Focke-Wulf FW190 just to the west of Compiegne in France. He continued to serve with No. 412 Squadron at Biggin Hill until 8 April 1944 when he returned to Canada. Beurling retired from the RCAF in October 1944 having found it difficult to settle back into the somewhat 'peacetime' way of life back in Canada. His life came to a tragic and abrupt end in May 1948 when an aircraft he was ferrying across Europe to Israel blew up after taking off from Rome; sabotage was suspected. At the time of his death George Beurling was just twenty-six years old.

On 5 January 1944 No. 412 Squadron went to Hutton Cranswick for two weeks to take part in an armament practice camp where the pilots were given bombing practice. The following day Spitfires of Nos 401 and 411 Squadrons provided the fighter sweep for medium bombers of No. 2 group detailed to attack 'Noball' targets. The formation was attacked and the Biggin Spitfires shot down two Focke-Wulf FW190s.

One Canadian pilot who would enjoy his first success during early 1944 was twenty-eight-year-old Flying Officer Bob Hayward. Born in Newfoundland, Hayward had joined the RCAF in 1940 and came to the UK at the end of 1942. He joined No. 401 Squadron RCAF in March 1943 and served with the squadron until just before D-Day, by which time he had been made a flight commander. During a *Ranger* sortie with the squadron on 11 February, he shot down a Messerschmitt Me210 whilst it was taking off from the *Luftwaffe*'s airfield at St Andre. A month later he would add a Focke-Wulf FW190 to his tally and during the following three months he would bring his total to five, having been transferred to No. 411 Squadron RCAF as a flight commander. He was then given command of the squadron in August 1944.

On 7 March pilots of No. 401 Squadron RCAF were escorting B-26s detailed to attack the railway marshalling yards at Creil when they encountered Focke-Wulf FW190s. During the following air combat two pilots from the squadron each shot down a FW190. One of the successful pilots was Flight Lieutenant Jack Sheppard from British Columbia. Sheppard had served with the squadron for a year and had been a flight commander for nine months. The FW190 he shot down to the north of Beaumont-sur-Oise was his second kill of the war. The other squadron pilot to enjoy success on 7 March was twenty-one-year-old Flying Officer Bill Klersy from Ontario. Klersy had joined the RCAF in 1941 and arrived in the UK in June

1943, being posted straight to No. 401 Squadron RCAF. The FW190 he shot down on 7 March was his first success of the war but not his last. By the end of the war Klersy would be one of the RCAF's top-scoring aces with fourteen confirmed victories plus dozens of vehicles and trains destroyed on the ground. This was a remarkable achievement in the space of just over a year. He was awarded the DFC and bar for his achievement and given command of the squadron in January 1945. Sadly, however, Bill Klersy was killed during a training sortie just days after the war was over; he was just twenty-three years old. The announcement of the award of the DSO followed soon after his death.

No. 401 Squadron RCAF enjoyed a successful morning on 15 March when the squadron joined forces with Canadian Spitfires from Kenley to escort more than seventy B-26s detailed to attack the railway marshalling yards at Aulnoy. The Biggin Hill pilots encountered a formation of Focke-Wulf FW190s trying to land at an airfield near Cambrai. The Canadians immediately swooped on the FW190s and in the space of just a few minutes managed to shoot down four. One of the Canadian pilots to be credited with one of the FW190s was Flight Lieutenant Jack Sheppard, his third FW190 kill of the war.

On 12 April command of No. 126 Airfield's squadrons was handed over from Wing Commander 'Buck' McNair to Wing Commander George Keefer who had been in command of No. 412 Squadron RCAF; in turn, Flight Lieutenant Jack Sheppard was promoted to take over command of the squadron. For 'Buck' McNair his operational flying was over. He had been credited with sixteen confirmed kills and when he left Biggin Hill McNair was awarded the DSO to add to his previously earned DFC and bar. McNair initially returned to Canada on leave but later returned to the UK to take up an appointment in the RCAF Overseas HQ, which he held until the end of the war.

The V-1 attacks against London during the early months of 1944 meant that Biggin Hill was dangerously in the line of fire; indeed, six V-1s came down within the airfield's boundary in a short period of time. Therefore, it was considered too risky to continue flying operations from Biggin Hill and so the decision was made for the squadrons to leave. The first to leave was No. 412 Squadron, which left Biggin at the end of March and moved to Fairwood Common near Swansea. It returned briefly on 7 April before leaving Biggin

Hill for the last time on 15 April when it moved to Tangmere. Within a week the other two squadrons had also left Biggin and joined No. 412 Squadron at Tangmere; No. 401 Squadron arrived at Tangmere on 17 April and No. 411 Squadron on 22 April. All three Canadian squadrons flew operational sorties in support of D-Day from Tangmere and the three squadrons were amongst the first air units to cross the Channel and operate from French soil, initially operating from Beny-sur-Mer (otherwise known as B.4). As part of No. 83 Group, the three squadrons then saw much action in the summer skies over Normandy before moving to Holland in September 1944, after which all three squadrons continued to operate from various airfields in mainland Europe until the end of the war. On 15 April, No. 126 Airfield moved from Biggin Hill to Tangmere and the station was taken over by Balloon Command.

By the end of 1944 it was considered safe enough to resume flying operations at Biggin Hill and so Balloon Command moved out and the squadrons moved back in. The last months of the war saw fighters carrying out fighter escort missions for Bomber Command's daylight raids over Europe. By the end of the war the airfield was increasingly used by transport aircraft and Biggin Hill was then officially transferred to Transport Command.

Having been transferred yet again, to Reserve Command in August 1946, Biggin Hill was transferred back to Fighter Command in 1949. Throughout the 1950s Biggin was home to the RAF's new jet fighters but the airfield's close proximity to London, and the increasingly crowded airspace in south-east England, meant that the RAF ceased flying operations in 1958. Biggin Hill was then divided into two with the RAF retaining the north side of the airfield and the south side was leased to Surrey Aviation for private flying. The RAF's side, known as North Camp, accommodated the Officers' Selection Centre, which opened in 1959 and then became the Aircrew Selection Centre in 1962. The south side, South Camp, received a boost in operations when nearby Croydon Airport closed in 1959 and many of its operators moved to Biggin Hill. The airfield was taken over by Bromley Council in 1973, which left the RAF's buildings of North Camp being used for selection. In 1979 the Government took the decision to close down RAF Biggin Hill with the exception of the Officers' Mess and St George's Chapel, although it was not until 1992 that the RAF finally moved out when the Officers' and Aircrew Selection Centre moved to RAF Cranwell.

The airfield at Biggin Hill has since been renamed as London Biggin Hill Airport. The airport has been upgraded for the operation of small commercial airliners and business jets, which also includes the construction of a passenger terminal and a new hangar.

Biggin Hill is located 6 miles to the south-east of Croydon, on the A233 Bromley–Westerham Road, and is very easy to find as it is well signposted. If travelling from the M25, exit at Junction 4 and take the A21 towards Bromley and then the A232. At the crossroads known as 'Keston Mark' turn left towards Westerham on the A233 and continue southwards for just over a mile when you will arrive at the site of the airfield. If approaching from the south then you will need to travel north up either the A21 or A22, if approaching from either the Tunbridge Wells or East Grinstead areas, and immediately before the M25 turn onto the A25 (left from the A21 or right from the A22). At Westerham turn on to the A233, this runs north towards Bromley. You will arrive at Biggin Hill after about 4 miles but remember that the order of description below will be reversed.

When arriving at Biggin Hill on the A233 from the north, the first part of the airfield reached is the main entrance to Biggin Hill Airport to the left. There is a barrier, which prevents entry to the site

A Hurricane and Spitfire outside the St George's Chapel of Remembrance at Biggin Hill. The chapel is open to visitors.

unless you have reason to do so or you have prior permission. If you are just visiting the site, there is little to see at this point. However, continuing towards Westerham there is more to see of this historic airfield. The road passes through the original site of RAF Biggin Hill and St George's Chapel of Remembrance can be seen on the left. It is well worth stopping at this point as this is where you will best capture the history of this famous site. Access to the St George's Chapel of Remembrance is through a gate at the front of the chapel, which is appropriately guarded by a Spitfire and Hurricane.

The original station church was destroyed by fire in 1946 but the chaplain at the time, the Reverend King, had the idea to build a permanent memorial chapel to commemorate all the Allied aircrew who gave their lives whilst operating from Biggin Hill during the Second World War. A grant from the Air Ministry, together with many personal donations, ensured that building soon began; most appropriately, the foundation stone was laid by Lord Dowding. The Chapel of Remembrance was dedicated by the Bishop of Rochester on 10 November 1951. The design retained the internal brick appearance of the original station church and the chapel is ornately furnished. The main features include twelve stained-glass windows, which have been donated by various organisations and individuals. Each is to a common theme, the Cloud of Witnesses, and depicts the spirit of a pilot holding a squadron badge of one of the seven squadrons that served at Biggin Hill or of Fighter Command or one of its groups. In addition to the general theme the windows contain some interesting detail. Those at the west end immortalise the Spitfire and Hurricane, and the second window from the back on the northern side has a mosquito insect painted in the lower right-hand corner; this is because the glazier flew Mosquitos during the Second World War. One of the windows was given by an anonymous donor and bears the inscription 'And some there be who have no memorial'. The west window in the St George's Room was installed as part of the fortieth anniversary of the Battle of Britain and the remaining four windows in the room were installed in 1985 to commemorate the part played by the ground trades of the RAF. Of particular interest are the three military medals in the lower right-hand corner of the Ground Control window, which were awarded to three members of the WAAF following their bravery during two attacks on the airfield

Biggin Hill is still very active as an airport and for private flying.

during the Battle of Britain. The gilded wooden eagle on the large lectern was privately donated and the small wooden lectern was donated by the Belgian Air Force. No. 92 Squadron's standard is also displayed in the chapel and the bible on the altar is believed to have come from the original station church, having been found on the site when it was cleared in 1949.

The Memorial Chapel is still within the community and is open daily to visitors between 10.00 a.m. and 4.00 p.m., although occasionally times may vary depending on the chapel's use and availability. There are weekly services, as well as special services of remembrance on Battle of Britain Sunday in September and Remembrance Day in November.

Continuing along the A233 southwards towards Westerham, the airfield can be clearly seen on the left. Biggin Hill is still one of the most popular light aviation venues south of London. At the mini-roundabout turn left to reach the private flying clubs that continue to use the airfield. These flying clubs provide everything from both light aircraft and helicopter-flying lessons to pleasure trips and many other services.

Squadron	Dates at Biggin Hill	Aircraft Type
401 Squadron RCAF	12 Oct 1943 – 7 Apr 1944	Spitfire IX
411 Squadron RCAF	13 Oct 1943 – 15 Apr 1944	Spitfire IX
412 Squadron RCAF	13 Oct 1943 – 15 Apr 1944	Spitfire IX

Fairlop

Known originally as Hainault Farm, the airfield of Fairlop rarely receives the recognition it deserves. During the winter of 1943–4 Fairlop was designated No. 136 Airfield as part of No. 84 Group 2nd TAF and was home to Hurricanes and Typhoons of No. 20 Wing. Flying ceased towards the end of the war and there are few reminders today of this former airfield.

The history of Fairlop airfield dates back to the First World War when the site was formerly known as Hainault Farm, named after the farm on which the airfield was developed. The village of Hainault is on the eastern side of London, to the south of Chigwell and west of Romford, and lies between the M11 and A12 major roads. The first aircraft to operate from the site were BE2s of No. 39 Squadron in 1916, which provided home defence for London against the Zeppelin airships. After the First World War the site was

Fairlop was home to Hurricane IVs during the early weeks of 1944, serving with No. 164 Squadron, and carried out rocket and bombing attacks in northern France. However, the heavily armed Hurricanes suffered in terms of performance in the operational theatre compared with other fighter-bombers.

surplus to requirements and the airfield closed; the land reverted to agriculture. There was a plan during the 1930s to develop the land as an airport for London but this idea was soon overtaken by events as the nation once more prepared for war.

During 1940 the land was developed once more for use as an airfield. It now adopted the name Fairlop, named after the village nearby, and was developed as a satellite for Hornchurch. The first unit to operate from the new site during the Second World War was No. 603 Squadron, equipped with Spitfires, which moved in from Hornchurch on 12 November 1941. Many fighter squadrons came and went from Fairlop during 1942 and the first half of 1943.

By the summer of 1943 there was one resident Mustang squadron at Fairlop, No. 239 Squadron, but this squadron moved north in August. Fairlop was then home to two Polish Spitfire squadrons during August and September but these two units only remained for a few weeks. They were replaced by Hurricanes of No. 164 Squadron and Typhoons of No. 195 Squadron. These two squadrons then became No. 136 Airfield 2nd TAF. The Hurricane IVs of No. 164 Squadron carried out rocket and bombing attacks in northern

The old oak tree standing in the middle of the roundabout outside the Fairlop Oak pub marks the location of the original airfield.

France but the heavily armed Hurricanes suffered in terms of performance in the operational theatre compared with other fighters; this led to the squadron re-equipping with Typhoons from January 1944.

The Typhoons of No. 195 Squadron carried out a variety of roles whilst operating from Fairlop, such as *Rhubarbs*, anti-shipping strikes and bomber escort missions. The two squadrons operated together from Fairlop until February 1944 when No. 195 Squadron disbanded and No. 164 Squadron moved to Twinwood Farm. The squadrons were replaced by another Typhoon unit, No. 193 Squadron, which moved in from Harrowbeer on 20 February 1944. However, this squadron only stayed at Fairlop for three weeks before moving on to Thorney Island.

This brought an end to operational flying from Fairlop as all squadrons were now moving south closer to the Channel to play their part in the forthcoming Allied invasion of Europe. After the D-Day operations were complete, Fairlop became home to a number of balloon squadrons until the end of the war; the airfield finally closed in 1946. The site was then used for a variety of

Whilst this view gives no indication that the site was once used as an airfield, Fairlop Waters gives a good idea of where the airfield once was. Walking around the park it is possible to find some evidence that the site was previously used as an airfield.

purposes before it became a country park known as Fairlop Waters with a lake, sailing club and golf course, which marks the area of the former airfield. In June 2002 Fairlop was overflown by aircraft of the RAF, as well as Concorde, which were taking part in the Queen's Golden Jubilee flypast over London.

The site of the former airfield can be found near the village of Barkingside to the north of the A12 and to the east of the A123 on the eastern outskirts of London. An old oak tree, known as the Fairlop Oak, stands on the roundabout at the Fairlop Oak pub. This has replaced the original noble oak tree that marked the original site of the airfield. The best area to visit the former airfield is at Fairlop Waters, which can be best reached by picking up the A12 Eastern Avenue eastwards from the A406 North Circular Road and travelling towards Junction 28 of the M25. After crossing the A123 continue along the A12 Eastern Avenue for another two miles. At some traffic lights there is a turning left, which is Hainault Road. As a check, the West Ham United Football Academy is on your immediate right at Little Heath. Just past the football academy keep left and continue along Hainault Road through an industrial area for about two miles. At the T-junction turn left into Forest Road, which leads towards Barkingside. The lake of Fairlop Waters is on your left after just less than a mile.

It is possible to park the car and take a walk but the lake now dominates the site, although there is the occasional area of concrete to give a reminder that an airfield was once there. Nineteen servicemen who died whilst serving at Fairlop during the Second World War are buried in the cemetery at Barkingside.

Squadron	Dates at Fairlop	Aircraft Type
239 Squadron	21 Jun – 14 Aug 43	Mustang I
302 'Poznanski' Squadron	19 Aug – 18 Sep 43	Spitfire V
317 'Wilenski' Squadron	21 Aug – 21 Sep 43	Spitfire V
164 Squadron	22 Sep 43 – 11 Feb 44	Hurricane IV & Typhoon I
195 Squadron	23 Sep 43 – 15 Feb 44	Typhoon I
193 Squadron	20 Feb – 15 Mar 44	Typhoon I

Heston

Originally used for civil aviation during the 1930s, Heston was designated No. 133 Airfield as part of No. 84 Group, 2nd TAF, during the winter of 1943–4 and was home to Spitfires of No. 18 Wing. Flying ceased at the end of the war as the development of Heathrow Airport dominated the local area. The M4 now passes through the site and Heston Services provides an indication of where the airfield once was.

The airfield of Heston was located about 15 miles to the west of London, just to the north of Hounslow. The origins of this airfield date back to 1929 when it was developed and subsequently used for civil aviation during the 1930s. It was at Heston on 30 September 1938 that the Prime Minister, Neville Chamberlain, famously showed off his piece of paper to the press and public following his return from Munich after his meeting with Adolf Hitler. He later stood outside Number 10 Downing Street and said that for the second time in our history, a British Prime Minister had returned from Germany bringing peace with honour!

At the outbreak of the Second World War the RAF requisitioned the site as a satellite for Northolt and it was used during the Battle of Britain by No. 1 Photographic Reconnaissance Unit (PRU) under the command of Wing Commander Geoffrey Tuttle. The unit operated eleven high-altitude Spitfires with the task of locating invasion barges across the Channel – a role that proved very successful, particularly during the period of late August and early September. The airfield was certainly considered an important enough target by the Germans as the *Luftwaffe* included Heston amongst its RAF airfield targets.

After the Battle of Britain, Heston was transferred to No. 81 Group. During 1941 the airfield was home to No. 53 Operational Training Unit and then No. 61 Operational Training Unit. In April 1942 Heston was transferred back to No. 11 Group and the airfield was upgraded from a satellite airfield to full station status. The first fighter squadron to arrive was the Polish No. 316 'Warszawski' Squadron, which arrived at Heston on 22 April 1942. A number of Polish fighter squadrons came and went from Heston during the next year as two Polish squadrons at Heston operated alongside two Polish squadrons based at Northolt as the Polish Wing.

The two resident Polish squadrons on 19 August, the day of the famous Dieppe Raid, were No. 302 'Poznanski' Squadron, under the command of Squadron Leader Jan Kowalski, and No. 308 'Krakowski' Squadron, under the command of Squadron Leader Walerian Zak; both squadrons took part in operations very early in the day but neither scored any success, nor did they suffer any losses.

In addition to the Polish fighter squadrons, No. 116 Squadron had also moved to Heston during April 1942 for calibration of anti-aircraft radar defences. The squadron operated a number of different types, such as Lysanders, Tiger Moths, Oxfords and even Hurricanes, and spent much of the time detached in small numbers to different airfields. The squadron remained at Heston until December 1943. Other units to use the airfield during 1943 were American transport units and these were frequent users of the airfield until the D-Day operations and beyond.

On 21 September 1943 Nos 306 'Torunski' and 308 'Krakowski' Squadrons arrived at Heston from Friston, although the latter squadron only remained at Heston until the end of October. Two weeks later No. 315 'Deblinski' Squadron arrived from Ballyhalbert. As part of the re-organisation of the structure within No. 84 Group, Heston was numbered No. 133 Airfield with effect from 1 November 1943. The two Polish squadrons then operated from Heston together until the spring of 1944. No. 306 'Torunski' Squadron was initially commanded at Heston by Squadron Leader Wlodzimierz Karwowski but command was handed over to Squadron Leader Stanislaw Lapka in January 1944. Both these pilots were veterans of the Battle of Britain. When No. 315 'Deblinski' Squadron arrived at Heston, the squadron was commanded by another Battle of Britain veteran, Squadron Leader Jerzy Poplawski.

The squadrons were initially involved in offensive operations across the Channel but the weather during November and December saw a reduction in operational sorties flown by the squadrons. On 29 November the two Heston squadrons were amongst a large escort package for more than seventy B-26 Marauders, which were detailed to attack the Belgian airfield of Chièvres. The formation was attacked by Focke-Wulf FW190s but the Polish pilots from Heston managed to fend off the attacking FW190s, claiming one FW190 destroyed.

The pace did pick up for the Heston squadrons during early 1944. On 15 February Squadron Leader Eugeniusz Horbaczewski took command of No. 315 Squadron. One of Poland's greatest fighter pilots of the Second World War, Horbaczewski was actually born in Russia but had joined the Polish Air Force in 1937. Having escaped to England soon after the outbreak of war, he was posted to No. 303 Squadron at the end of 1940. His first aerial success did not come until a year later but the Messerschmitt Bf109 he claimed near Nieuport was only ever officially considered to be a 'probable' kill. Horbaczewski had to wait until April 1942 to be credited with his first kill – a Focke-Wulf FW190 between St Omer and Calais. Horbaczewski was then posted to the Desert Air Force in 1943 where he flew Spitfire IXs with No. 145 Squadron.

Further successes quickly followed, including five kills in the space of just four weeks. He returned to the UK in February 1944 to take command of No. 315 Squadron at Heston, by which time he had been credited with eleven kills. Although he would leave Heston with his squadron at the beginning of April, Horbaczewski led his squadron throughout the D-Day operations and the period immediately after. Sadly, however, he was killed on 18 August during a mass air combat with an estimated sixty Focke-Wulf FW190s over Beauvais. Although Horbaczewski was credited with shooting down three of the FW190s, his luck ran out and he was shot down and killed.

Heston Services on the M4 gives an idea of where the former airfield once was. In the background an airliner appropriately makes its final approach to the westerly runway at Heathrow.

By March 1944 No. 315 'Deblinski' Squadron was starting its conversion to Mustang IIIs. On 16 March No. 129 Squadron arrived at Heston having been moved south from Scotland to re-join 2nd TAF. This briefly brought the strength at No. 133 Airfield up to three squadrons, although No. 129 Squadron started to take delivery of Mustang IIIs towards the end of the month and the squadron then left Heston for its Armament Practice Camp at Llanbedr in Wales before moving to Coolham ready for the D-Day operations.

The final build-up towards the Allied invasion of Europe meant that all fighter squadrons were required further south where they could operate within range of the landing beaches. As such, No. 133 Airfield, including both squadrons, left Heston for Coolham on 1 April. The following month, No. 85 Group's Communications Squadron moved into Heston, operating different types of aircraft such as Oxfords and Austers.

Heston remained an active airfield for the remainder of the Second World War and further improvements to the airfield's facilities were made before the end of hostilities. Although there were plans for the further development of Heston after the war, flying ceased in 1946. The development of Heathrow Airport then dominated the local area and the site of the former airfield at Heston was developed for housing and commercial business; many of the local roads have names relating to the history of aviation. The M4 now passes through the centre of this former airfield where the Heston Services, just to the east of Junction 3, marks the area.

Squadron	Dates at Heston	Aircraft Type
116 Squadron	20 Apr 42 – 12 Dec 43	Lysander/Oxford/Tiger Moth/Hurricane
302 'Poznanski' Squadron	1 – 20 Jun 43	Spitfire V
317 'Wilenski' Squadron	1 – 21 Jun 43	Spitfire V
308 'Krakowski' Squadron	21 Sep – 29 Oct 43	Spitfire V
306 'Torunski' Squadron	21 Sep 43 – 1 Apr 44	Spitfire V & Mustang III
315 'Deblinski' Squadron	13 Nov 43 – 1 Apr 44	Spitfire V & IX
129 Squadron	16 – 30 Mar 44	Spitfire IX

Hornchurch

A famous fighter airfield, the origins of Hornchurch date back to the First World War. Following the formation of 2nd TAF, Hornchurch was designated No. 135 Airfield as part of No. 84 Group and was home to Spitfire squadrons of No. 20 Wing during the winter of 1943–4. Hornchurch was used by the RAF until 1962 and the site is now Hornchurch Country Park.

Formerly known as Sutton's Farm, the site of this famous RAF fighter airfield can be found on the eastern side of London on what is now Hornchurch Country Park. The origins of the airfield date back to the First World War when Sutton's Farm was first used by the Royal Flying Corps in 1915. One heroic act took place on the night of 2/3 September 1916 when twenty-one-year-old William Leefe Robinson, a BE2c pilot serving with No. 39 Squadron, brought down a German Zeppelin airship over London. The Zeppelin was one of sixteen taking part in the largest airship raid of the war and the act was witnessed by hundreds of locals. Having been subject to many Zeppelin raids, this helped raise the morale of the local population. For this heroic act William Leefe Robinson was awarded the Victoria Cross.

When the First World War ended the newly formed RAF decided not to retain the airfield of Sutton's Farm. However, that decision was reversed in 1928 and the airfield re-opened as RAF Hornchurch. During the 1930s Hornchurch was home to a number of fighter squadrons. In 1936, as part of the RAF's restructuring, Hornchurch became part of No. 11 Group, Fighter Command, and there then followed much development work to improve the airfield facilities during the final months before the Second World War.

Following the German advance into France and the Low Countries the Hornchurch fighter squadrons became involved in the air war over France and the subsequent Battle of Britain. During the Battle of Britain itself, Hornchurch was one of Fighter Command's key Sector airfields and throughout the battle it was home to a number of Spitfire squadrons. To complete the Battle of Britain line-up during the summer of 1940, Blenheims of No. 600 Squadron operated from Hornchurch for three weeks during the end of August and early September, and Defiants of No. 264

Squadron briefly operated from the airfield for a few days at the end of August.

Hornchurch was also home to many famous fighter pilots during the Battle of Britain. To name just a few of the few, Squadron Leader 'Sailor' Malan, a South African, commanded No. 74 Squadron from August 1940; Malan ended the war with twenty-seven confirmed kills and was awarded the DSO and bar and the DFC and bar. Another of Fighter Command's finest to have flown from the airfield during the battle was the New Zealander Al Deere who was a flying officer serving with No. 54 Squadron during the Battle of Britain. By the end of August 1940 Al Deere had scored fourteen victories and when he left Hornchurch the following month he was awarded a bar to his DFC; Al Deere ended the war with twenty confirmed victories, although his actual score could well have been higher. Also serving at Hornchurch during the Battle of Britain was Warrant Officer 'Tubby' Mayne of No. 74 Squadron, who at the age of thirty-nine was the oldest pilot to fly as a regular squadron pilot during the battle. The list could go on and on and the stories of individual acts of bravery of the few and devastating losses at Hornchurch could be the subject of a book on their own. As for the airfield itself, Hornchurch was an obvious target for the *Luftwaffe* during the summer of 1940. There were some twenty raids against Hornchurch during the Battle of Britain, with the heaviest and most devastating raid occurring during the early afternoon of 31 August when the airfield was attacked by sixty Dornier Do17s of KG2.

After the Battle of Britain, various squadrons were based at Hornchurch as part of the Hornchurch Wing, which took part in various fighter sweeps across the Channel. During 1941 the airfield's facilities were improved to accommodate additional aircraft and this development work included the construction of dispersal sites. At the beginning of 1942 the Hornchurch Wing consisted of three Spitfire V squadrons: No. 64 Squadron under the command of Squadron Leader Bryan Wicks, No. 313 (Czechoslovak) Squadron under the command of Squadron Leader Karl Mrazek and No. 411 Squadron RCAF under the command of Squadron Leader Stan Turner. This was, indeed, an impressive line-up and Hornchurch was home to some experienced commanding officers, flight commanders and other senior pilots within the squadrons.

In June Wing Commander Paddy Finucane arrived at

Hornchurch to take command of the Hornchurch Wing. Finucane was born in Dublin and was a veteran of the Battle of Britain, having served with No. 65 Squadron. He was awarded the DFC in May 1941 having achieved five confirmed kills. He was then posted as a flight commander with No. 452 Squadron RAAF at Kenley and during the period August to October 1941 Finucane added a further seventeen confirmed kills plus many more claimed as 'probable' or 'damaged'. This outstanding achievement earned Paddy Finucane two bars to his DFC and the award of the DSO. In January 1942 Finucane was given command of No. 602 Squadron at Redhill. Whilst commanding No. 602 Squadron, Finucane took his total score to twenty-six confirmed kills. However, tragedy struck on 15 July 1942 when Finucane was leading the Hornchurch Wing over northern France. His Spitfire was hit by ground fire and then his engine seized whilst crossing the Channel in an attempt to reach southern England. Finucane attempted to ditch in the Channel but his aircraft was seen to sink before Finucane could escape the cockpit. Finucane was, indeed, one of the most gallant fighter pilots to have served at Hornchurch. At the time of his death, Paddy Finucane was just twenty-one years old.

The Hornchurch squadrons were involved in the famous Dieppe Raid on 19 August 1942. The three squadrons operating from the airfield at that time were Nos 64, 122 and 340 (Free French) Squadrons. No. 64 Squadron, in particular, had a successful day; the squadron claimed seven enemy aircraft destroyed but, unfortunately, lost two pilots killed. One pilot of No. 64 Squadron to enjoy success that day was Flight Lieutenant Don Kingaby. The Dornier Do217 that he shot down to the south of Dieppe was his eighteenth confirmed kill of the war. The son of a vicar, and initially a sergeant pilot, Don Kingaby was the only man to have been awarded the DFM and two bars; he was just twenty-one years old at the time.

During 1943 the Hornchurch Wing continued operations across the Channel. Many squadrons came and went throughout the year but the two mainstay squadrons from June until the end of 1943 were Nos 222 and 129 Squadrons, both Spitfire IX squadrons. Although a totally Spitfire wing, Hornchurch was briefly home to Mustangs of No. 239 Squadron during August and September but the squadron's stay was for only a matter of weeks.

Commanding Hornchurch during this period was Wing

Commander David Scott-Malden who had taken command of the station in October 1943. A former graduate of Cambridge University, Scott-Malden had joined the RAF following the outbreak of the Second World War. No stranger to the station, Scott-Malden had previously commanded No. 54 Squadron at Hornchurch during 1941.

On 29 November the Spitfires of No. 129 Squadron were helping to provide fighter escort for a package of more than seventy B-26 Marauders, which were detailed to attack the Belgian airfield of Chièvres. The formation was attacked by Focke-Wulf FW190s and during the following combat pilots of No. 129 Squadron shot down two of the FW190s.

By January 1944 both No. 222 Squadron and No. 129 Squadron had left Hornchurch. Between January and May 1944 Hornchurch was used by ten different Spitfire squadrons but none remained for more than a month. One of the pilots serving with No. 66 Squadron at Hornchurch during this period was twenty-three-year-old Flying Officer Arthur Varey. Born in Hull, Varey had joined the RAF in 1940 and had distinguished himself whilst flying Spitfires in Malta with No. 126 Squadron. During 1942 he made many claims, although not all could be officially confirmed as many aircraft would have come down unwitnessed in the Mediterranean. He was, however, still credited with five confirmed kills plus many more officially listed as 'probables' and 'damaged'. As a flight sergeant, he was awarded the DFM at the end of the year. Varey then returned to the UK and was commissioned. He joined No. 66 Squadron in April 1943 and had his first success with the squadron during October. On 9 February 1944 he had a lucky escape whilst flying with the squadron in the Gournay area. He and his wingman were bounced by eight Focke-Wulf FW190s and during the following combat his aircraft was hit. Fortunately Varey and his wingman survived the encounter although both Spitfires were badly damaged. Arthur Varey survived the war, after which he returned to Hull.

During the early hours of 23 February, some bombs fell on Hornchurch, which caused severe destruction and damage to fifteen Spitfires of No. 504 Squadron. Who dropped these bombs is unclear. Command of No. 135 Airfield had now passed from Wing Commander Roy Marples to Wing Commander Peter Simpson. Already a 'veteran' Simpson had just celebrated his twenty-third

A Spitfire and ground crew of No. 222 Squadron at Hornchurch in early 1944.

birthday just a few days before taking command. Simpson had joined the RAF just before the outbreak of the Second World War. He had initially flown Hurricanes with No. 111 Squadron during the evacuation of Dunkirk and he then flew Spitfires with No. 64 Squadron during the Battle of Britain before returning again to No. 111 Squadron. Awarded the DFC at the end of 1940 he later commanded both No. 130 Squadron and No. 504 Squadron before he was given command at Hornchurch. Commanding No. 349 (Belgian) Squadron was Squadron Leader Count Yvan Du Monceau de Bergandael, one of the highest scoring Belgian fighter pilots of the war.

As the Allied invasion was now drawing nearer, the squadrons based furthest from the Channel were moved to bases along the south coast. On 11 April, No. 135 Airfield moved from Hornchurch to Selsey and one by one the squadrons left Hornchurch for bases further south. The last three squadrons left Hornchurch on 19 May 1944. Hornchurch had done its job. The war was effectively over for this famous fighter airfield, which had played such a vital role in Britain's defence during 1940 and for the next four years as the RAF took the offensive back across the Channel. The operations room was closed down and most buildings were empty as the Allied advance into Europe began. The V-1 flying bomb threat to London during the late summer of 1944 brought an end to wartime fighter operations from Hornchurch altogether, as the construction of many local defences meant that flying from the airfield was too hazardous. For the last six months of the war Hornchurch was used as a marshalling base for Service personnel transiting to and from operational theatres.

After the war Hornchurch was placed on care and maintenance, although a Reserve flying school did continue to operate from the site until 1953. Hornchurch was then used as the RAF's Aircrew Selection Centre before the station finally closed in 1962. The land was then sold and the site became a quarry and later a refuse tip. It has now been developed for housing and is the site of the Hornchurch Country Park, which covers an extensive area and is full of attractive wild life. The airfield's buildings have long been demolished, although some reminders of this once famous airfield can still be found.

The site is large but not immediately obvious when finding it for the first time. It can be found by going northwards from the A1306 along the A125 Rainham to Hornchurch road. After 1 mile there is a sign for the Hornchurch Country Park to the right. Take this turning and after another mile or so, turn right at a set of traffic lights; this is Airfield Way. The road will take you down towards the Country Park and marks what was once a perimeter track, which also follows the line of where the hangars once stood. You will notice the names of the roads in the area relate to the RAF and the road

Hornchurch Country Park now dominates the site of the former airfield.

leading down to the Country Park is called Squadron's Approach. On arriving at the car park the first thing to note is that this was a former aircraft dispersal and blast pen. The best thing to do then is to take a walk around the site and look across the area whilst imagining life as it would have been during the Second World War. The sound of aircraft and the flurry of activity have all been replaced by the serene setting, nature's own sounds and the vast array of wild life in the Country Park.

One of the local schools on the adjacent housing estate is named the R.J. Mitchell Primary School, appropriately named after the designer of the Spitfire; the school can be found in Tangmere Crescent. The school marks the location of the former administration site and specifically where the Station Headquarters once stood. In 2003 the RAF presented the local council with a Battle of Britain diptych, which contains the names of 2,000 personnel who served at Hornchurch and it is embossed with the names of twelve surviving pilots who flew from the airfield. It is proudly displayed at Havering Town Hall.

Squadron	Dates at Hornchurch	Aircraft Type
453 Squadron RAAF	27 Mar – 28 Jun 43	Spitfire IX
222 Squadron	29 Apr 43 – 30 Dec 43	Spitfire IX
129 Squadron	28 Jun 43 – 17 Jan 44	Spitfire IX
239 Squadron	14 Aug – 30 Sep 43	Mustang I
485 Squadron RNZAF	18 Oct – 8 Nov 43	Spitfire V & IX
66 Squadron	8 Nov 43 – 23 Feb 44	Spitfire IX
350 (Belgian) Squadron	30 Dec 43 – 10 Mar 44	Spitfire IX
504 Squadron	19 Jan – 10 Mar 44	Spitfire V
485 Squadron RNZAF	28 Feb – 7 Apr 44	Spitfire IX
222 Squadron	10 Mar – 4 Apr 44	Spitfire IX
349 (Belgian) Squadron	11 Mar – 11 Apr 44	Spitfire IX
229 Squadron	24 Apr – 19 May 44	Spitfire IX
274 Squadron	24 Apr – 19 May 44	Spitfire IX
80 Squadron	6 – 19 May 44	Spitfire IX

Kenley

With its origins dating back to the First World War, Kenley is another famous RAF airfield that requires little or no introduction. During 1943–4 it was No. 127 Airfield as part of No. 83 Group, 2nd TAF, and was home to three Canadian squadrons of Spitfires. Post-war the station was used by the RAF until 1959 and the site is now Kenley Common, which is still used for gliding.

One of the RAF's most famous wartime airfields, Kenley was developed on land on Henley Common to the south of Croydon in Surrey. The site was first used as an airfield in 1917 when it was used as an aircraft acceptance park and for the remainder of the First World War, many aircraft and crews passed through the site on their way to operational units in France and Belgium.

The airfield was retained by the post-war RAF because of its facilities, although the wartime units were either disbanded or moved out. The first post-war flying unit to use the airfield was No. 24 Squadron, which re-formed at Kenley in April 1920 as a communications and training squadron, primarily providing air transport for the Government due to its close proximity to London. The squadron was joined by No. 32 Squadron, a single-seat fighter squadron, in April 1923. For nearly ten years this squadron operated a number of different aircraft at Kenley: Snipe (until December 1924), Grebe II (1924–7), Gamecock II (1926–8), Siskin III (1928–31) and finally the Bristol Bulldog (from 1930 until the squadron left in 1932). No. 24 Squadron was replaced by No. 23 Squadron, another fighter squadron, early in 1927 and Nos 23 and 32 Squadrons operated together from Kenley until 1932.

In September 1932 the two fighter squadrons left for Biggin Hill so that major reconstruction work could be carried out at Kenley. Work was completed in 1934 and Kenley was soon home to two more fighter squadrons, with Bristol Bulldogs of Nos 3 and 17 Squadrons arriving in May. These two squadrons operated from Kenley until 1939, although No. 3 Squadron did spend some time in the Middle East during 1935–6. During the final months before the Second World War there were several squadron movements in and out of Kenley and the airfield went through further reconstruction work. This included the construction of two runways; one of 1,000 yards and the other of 1,200 yards, and twelve concrete aircraft dispersal pens.

Kenley's location and close proximity to London meant that it was one of Fighter Command's main fighter airfields during the Battle of Britain. As the Sector airfield for the Kenley Sector, Kenley had the responsibility for airspace immediately to the south of London and covering the area between the Tangmere and Biggin Hill Sectors to the west and east respectively. When the Battle of Britain began Kenley was home to Spitfires of No. 64 Squadron and Hurricanes of No. 615 Squadron. Both squadrons were in action during the early days of the battle.

The first two weeks of August 1940 were particularly hectic for the Kenley squadrons and squadron activity peaked on 15 August when the squadrons flew nearly 100 sorties between them. Kenley was understandably a priority target for the *Luftwaffe* and the first attack on the airfield took place early in the afternoon of 18 August when Kenley was attacked by about fifty Do17s of KG76. The airfield suffered considerable damage with more than 100 bombs landing within the boundary. Three Hurricanes were destroyed on the ground and three hangars plus many more buildings were destroyed. The operations building was also put out of action and there was considerable damage to many other buildings and to the water and gas supplies. Nine of Kenley's personnel were killed during the raid and at least ten more injured.

Although it had been a disastrous day for Kenley many of the bombs dropped had been released from low level and, fortunately, had not exploded. This was probably due to Kenley's anti-aircraft defences, which were credited with bringing down one of the Do17s during the raid. The Dornier crashed on a private house in Golf Road just outside the airfield boundary; miraculously the owner survived, although the house was completely destroyed. The Dornier crew plus a German war correspondent on board were all killed. A second Dornier hit by the airfield's defences crashed near Biggin Hill and the crew were captured.

By 10 September Kenley was an all-Hurricane station with both Nos 253 and 501 Squadrons remaining as the station's resident squadrons for the remainder of the battle. This period was particularly difficult for No. 253 Squadron, which suffered the loss of five Hurricanes in two separate actions during its first day at Kenley. If this was not enough, the squadron also lost three commanding officers in just one week during September.

Many famous Battle of Britain pilots operated from Kenley

during the Battle of Britain but probably none more famous than Sergeant 'Ginger' Lacey who served with No. 501 Squadron. James Ginger Lacey had initially made his mark during the Battle of France and had then scored further successes during the early period of the Battle of Britain. By the time he arrived at Kenley he had already been credited with fifteen confirmed kills and had been awarded the DFM. By the time he left Kenley at the end of the battle, Ginger Lacey had taken his total to twenty-three confirmed kills, making him the highest RAF scoring pilot of the Battle of Britain for which he was awarded a bar to his DFM.

The Battle of Britain was undoubtedly the high point of Kenley's history. With the battle over the two Hurricane squadrons were both replaced by two more Hurricane squadrons, Nos 1 and 615 Squadrons, and both these units were involved in offensive operations over Northern France. During the latter half of 1941 the Hurricanes were replaced by Spitfires and by the end of the following year Kenley was home to the Canadian Wing, playing host to various RCAF squadrons.

On 19 August 1942 Kenley played a major part in the famous Dieppe Raid. At that time there were two squadrons of Spitifres based at Kenley including No. 111 Squadron, which was under the command of Squadron Leader Pete Wickham, a veteran of the First Libyan and Greece campaigns of 1940–41 for which he had been awarded the DFC and bar. Also based at Kenley for the Dieppe Raid was No. 402 Squadron RCAF, which had arrived from Redhill a week before the raid. Completing the international line-up was the USAAF's 308th Fighter Squadron, which was also operating Spitfires at that time.

The strong association between Kenley and the Canadians gained official recognition in November 1942 when the Canadians' Kenley Wing was formed. The wing consisted of a number of Canadian Spitfire squadrons at various times, which seemed to come and go from Kenley quite frequently. Noticeably from March 1943 the wing was commanded by Wing Commander Johnnie Johnson. Whilst leading the Kenley Wing between March and September 1943 Johnnie Johnson was credited with fifteen confirmed kills and several more claimed as probable or damaged. This was, indeed, an outstanding achievement and Johnnie Johnson was awarded the DSO and bar, to add to his previously earned DFC and bar.

On 12 July 1943 Kenley officially became No. 127 Airfield and was then designated as No. 127 Wing in August, which became part of No. 83 Group, 2nd TAF, on its formation. In August Spitfire Vs of No. 165 Squadron arrived at Kenley. It was the only non-Canadian unit at that time, although the squadron only stayed at Kenley for a month. From 14 October 1943 until the spring of 1944 there were just two resident squadrons at Kenley, both Canadian, Nos 403 and 421 RCAF Squadrons having returned from Headcorn. No. 403 Squadron RCAF was commanded by Squadron Leader Bob Buckham from Vancouver. Buckham had initially served as a sergeant pilot in the RCAF before he was commissioned in March 1942. He had scored his first success of the war during the Dieppe Raid on 19 August 1942 whilst serving with No. 416 Squadron, and had been given command of No. 403 Squadron RCAF on arrival at Kenley in October 1943.

Commanding No. 421 Squadron RCAF at Kenley during this period was Squadron Leader Charles Magwood. Born in Toronto, Magwood had joined the RCAF at the outbreak of the Second World

Spitfire IX of No. 403 Squadron RCAF during the early weeks of 1944.

War. He had scored his first success earlier in 1943 whilst serving with No. 403 Squadron RCAF. During two days in April 1943 Magwood had destroyed three Focke-Wulf FW190s over northern France for which he was awarded the DFC. He had been given command of No. 421 Squadron RCAF in October and remained until just before Christmas 1943 when he was posted to the overseas HQ of the RCAF.

Command of No. 421 Squadron RCAF was then given to Squadron Leader Wally Conrad and he would remain in command of the squadron until after D-Day. Conrad was twenty-three years old and was the son of a church minister from Ontario. Wally Conrad had made a name for himself whilst serving with No. 274 Squadron in the Middle East for which he was awarded the DFC. Conrad had returned to the UK in February 1943 and joined No. 403 Squadron. He then had a lucky escape in August when he collided with another Spitfire over France and had to bale out. Conrad managed to evade capture and returned to England two months later via Spain. Wally Conrad was then promoted and given command of No. 421 Squadron RCAF at Kenley.

On 20 December the Kenley Wing was airborne twice during the day to provide fighter escort for large formations of Marauders, Mitchells and Bostons detailed to attack Bremen. During the late morning Flying Officer Andy MacKenzie of No. 421 Squadron RCAF shot down two Focke-Wulf FW190s and a Messerschmitt Bf109 over the Merville-Douai area. MacKenzie had only joined the squadron just a matter of weeks before and had already claimed his first victory of the war during October. On this particular occasion he broke away from his flight to single-handedly attack a number of enemy fighters; the three confirmed kills of the encounter brought Andy MacKenzie an immediate DFC.

During the afternoon of 30 December, No. 403 Squadron RCAF was in action in the Compiegne area when they encountered a number of Messerschmitt Bf109s. The Canadians claimed two Bf109s destroyed, one of which was shot down to the south-east of Albert by a twenty-year-old American, Pilot Officer Claude Weaver III. This was Weaver's eleventh kill of the war. He had enlisted in the RCAF and came to the UK during 1942 and joined No. 412 Squadron RCAF as a sergeant pilot. Posted to Malta to join No. 185 Squadron, Weaver scored his first aerial success in July 1942. By the end of the summer he had taken his total to ten confirmed kills when he was shot down on 9 September and taken as a prisoner of war. Weaver managed to escape a year later and he then returned to the UK where he joined No. 403 Squadron RCAF. His eleventh kill on 30 December was followed by his twelfth on 21 January 1944 but sadly Claude Weaver was killed just a week later whilst on a Ranger sortie over the Amiens area. The award of a DFC was subsequently announced for this gallant young American to add to the DFM and bar he had so gallantly earned during the defence of Malta.

Both Canadian squadrons had a quiet start to 1944 and their involvement in operations was sporadic. No. 403 Squadron RCAF's main task during early 1944 was *Ramrods* and *Rangers* over Europe. It was a similar story for No. 421 Squadron RCAF, although this squadron was also increasingly used for attacks against V-1 sites. The number of squadrons at Kenley increased to three when No. 416 Squadron RCAF moved south from Digby and arrived at Kenley on 11 February. Kenley lost another of its gallant young Canadians during the morning of 8 March when Flying Officer Jim Ballantyne of No. 403 Squadron RCAF was shot down by ground defences near St Aurore de l'Eure. Ballantyne had previously served in Malta and was awarded the DFM, being commissioned at the end of 1942. He had then returned to Canada in 1943 but returned to the UK once more and joined No. 403 Squadron RCAF in January 1944.

The squadrons then began to work-up in dive-bombing tactics as the daily tempo gathered pace but none of the squadrons remained at Kenley during the final preparations for the Allied invasion of Europe. All three squadrons left Kenley for Tangmere during April and within two months the three Canadian squadrons would be operating together from Bazenville across the Channel. Command and control of Kenley had already been taken over by Biggin Hill in March 1944 and the airfield played no major operational role during the D-Day operations. Kenley was also closed during the period of V-1 rocket attacks against London during the summer months of 1944.

After the Second World War, Kenley was transferred to Transport Command and then to Reserve Command. During the 1950s the airfield was used in various movies such as *Angels One Five* and *Reach for the Sky*. RAF Kenley closed in 1959, although the airfield remained in use for gliding until it was finally placed on care and maintenance in 1966.

The 'Tribute to Kenley' Memorial has been erected on one of the former aircraft blast pens. It cannot be seen from the country lane but is signposted and can be found alongside Hayes Lane.

The airfield has remained until the present day and is used by the Surrey Gliding Club and No. 615 Volunteer Gliding School, which provides gliding experience for the Air Cadet Organisation and the Combined Cadet Forces of Surrey, Sussex, Kent and London. It is also home to No. 450 (Kenley) Squadron of the Air Cadets. Although most of the land is still owned by the Ministry of Defence, much of it is accessible to the public as Kenley Common. The airfield is situated between the A22 (to the east) and the B2030 (to its south and west) but is not particularly easy to find and could be easily missed by the casual passer-by when driving south on the A22 Croydon to Caterham road.

Probably the best way of finding the airfield is from the A23 London to Brighton road. To the south of Croydon take the A22 at Purley towards Caterham and then proceed through the village of Kenley. Turn right at the roundabout at the village of Whyteleafe towards the railway station. Continue along this road, crossing the railway line, and proceed up Whyteleafe Hill with St Luke's Church on the left. At the top of the hill turn right and this is the southern part of the airfield, which is used by the Surrey and Gliding Club and the Volunteer Gliding School. Some former buildings remain, including the Officers' Mess and the Sergeants' Mess. The local RAF

The runway at Kenley today.

Graves of RAF personnel from Kenley in the churchyard at St Luke's Church on Whyteleafe Hill.

Association meets in one of the station's former administration buildings. Continuing along the road around the western side of the airfield there is a tribute to Kenley Memorial. It is situated in one of the former aircraft blast pens and cannot be seen from the road but it is signposted from the road; it can easily be reached by parking the car and walking a matter of yards along the footpath. From the site of the memorial continue along the road, with the airfield on the right, and turn left from Hayes Lane into Old Lodge Lane; you will then reach the Wattenden Arms. This was a favourite local pub for those serving at Kenley during the Second World War and several pictures and reminders of life at the airfield can be seen. Returning to St Luke's Church at Whyteleafe Hill, it is worth stopping to spend a few minutes in the churchyard where there is a separate burial site for those killed whilst serving at Kenley; the site has the words 'To the perpetual memory of all those who served at Royal Air Force Kenley'.

Squadron	Dates at Kenley	Aircraft Type
403 Squadron RCAF	23 Jan – 7 Aug 43	Spitfire IX
421 Squadron RCAF	17 May – 6 Aug 43	Spitfire IX
165 Squadron	8 Aug – 17 Sep 43	Spitfire V
403 Squadron RCAF	14 Oct 43 – 18 Apr 44	Spitfire IX
421 Squadron RCAF	14 Oct 43 – 18 Apr 44	Spitfire IX
416 Squadron RCAF	11 Feb – 14 Apr 44	Spitfire IX

Northholt

The only airfield used by 2nd TAF during the D-Day operations and still in use by the RAF is Northolt. The airfield's origins date back more than ninety years and following the formation of 2nd TAF in 1943 Northolt was designated No. 131 Airfield of No. 84 Group and was home to three Polish Spitfire squadrons of No. 18 Wing. On D-Day Northolt was home to No. 34 (PR) Wing and its squadrons took part in many reconnaissance sorties during the Allied invasion of Europe.

RAF Northolt is situated about 15 miles to the west of London and can be found immediately on the north side of the A40 Western Avenue as you drive to or from London. The site of this famous RAF airfield was first considered for use as an aerodrome in 1910, during the very first days of powered flight. However, there was no development of the site until 1915 when Northolt was used by the Royal Flying Corps for home defence. Northolt was also used as a training airfield and from 1917 was also used by the Americans following the entry into the First World War of the United States.

After the war was over the training units disbanded and Northolt became a joint military and civil airfield. From 1923 until 1935 the airfield was home to No. 41 Squadron, which operated Snipes, Siskins, Bulldogs and Demons during its time at Northolt. During this period No. 24 Squadron also operated from Northolt, arriving in 1927 and leaving in 1933, during which time it operated various types of communications aircraft with the additional responsibility of flying senior RAF officers to and from the Air Ministry in London. Northolt was also briefly home to two Auxiliary Air Force squadrons during the mid-1920s.

In 1934 No. 111 Squadron, equipped with Bristol Bulldogs, arrived at Northolt and this squadron remained until the outbreak of the Second World War. The squadron had been joined in 1936 by No. 23 Squadron, equipped with Hawker Demons, and by the time war had been declared Northolt had transferred to No. 11 Group, Fighter Command. By then the airfield had been improved with two paved runways, 800 yards long, which meant that Northolt was one of the few RAF airfields to have hardened runways at the start of the war; it also boasted one of the early C-type hangars, which was amongst the first to have been built.

At the start of the Battle of Britain Northolt was home to Hurricanes of Nos 1 and 257 Squadrons. No. 303 Squadron formed at Northolt in July 1940 and was largely made up of Polish personnel evacuated from France. The squadron received its first Hurricanes at the end of the month and commenced training early in August. Because of the lack of English-speaking pilots the Poles were initially kept out of the front line but this changed on 30 August following a training flight over Hertfordshire. A young Polish pilot, Flying Officer Ludwig Paszkiewicz, spotted enemy bombers and transmitted his sighting to his formation leader, Squadron Leader Ronald Kellett. Paszkiewicz received no reply. Having frustratingly been kept out of the battle for so long, Paszkiewicz then attacked the Dornier Do17 alone and officially scored the squadron's first kill. Whilst this lack of discipline might not have been tolerated in normal circumstances, Air Chief Marshal Sir Hugh Dowding, Commander-in-Chief of Fighter Command, agreed that the Poles should immediately be declared operational. This decision proved instrumental during the Battle of Britain as the Poles went on to serve with distinction and extreme courage for the rest of the battle and, indeed, the war.

There were many examples of individual courage and determination during this key part of the station's long and distinguished history. One example was the courage shown by Group Captain Stanley Vincent, the station commander at Northolt during the Battle of Britain who flew operationally during the battle, often operating alone. He was credited with two confirmed Bf109s in September 1940. This made Stanley Vincent the only RAF pilot to have been credited with kills during both the First and Second World Wars, his previous kill having occurred in January 1917 over the Western Front.

Because of its location, Northolt did not suffer the devastating attacks experienced by other Fighter Command airfields but it was attacked twice during the latter weeks of the battle. There was also the tragic loss of Sergeant Josef Frantisek of No. 303 Squadron during a routine patrol on 8 October. Frantisek was a Czech pilot who had fought with the Polish and French forces earlier in the war. He had made his way across the Channel after the German advance through France and the Low Countries to continue the fight with the RAF. He had been an original member of No. 303 Squadron when it formed at Northolt and had destroyed seventeen enemy aircraft, which made Josef Frantisek the top scoring pilot during the Battle of Britain. This was a remarkable achievement considering his first success was on 2 September; his seventeen kills had come in the space of just five weeks. Josef Frantisek is buried in Northwood Cemetery, Middlesex.

After the Battle of Britain Northolt remained a Polish base and by mid-1941 all the squadrons based there were Polish. When nearby Heston gained satellite status in 1942, just two squadrons were based at Northolt with two more at Heston; together the four squadrons operated as the Polish Wing.

At the time 2nd TAF formed in November 1943, Northolt was home to three Polish Spitfire IX squadrons: No. 302 'Poznanski' Squadron and No. 317 'Wilenski' Squadron had both arrived from Fairlop in September, and they were joined the following month by No. 308 'Krakowski' Squadron, which had arrived from Heston. Northolt was then numbered as No. 131 Airfield and the three Northolt squadrons operated alongside the Heston squadrons as the 18th Fighter Wing under the command and control of No. 84 Group, 2nd TAF.

Whilst at Northolt, No. 302 Squadron was under the command of twenty-eight-year-old Squadron Leader Waclaw Krol. Like many other Polish pilots, Krol was serving with the Polish Air Force when the Germans invaded Poland on 1 September 1939. Having escaped Poland via Rumania, Krol also served with the French before finally crossing the Channel where he joined the RAF. Krol was one of the few Polish pilots to have confirmed kills with the Polish, French and Royal Air Forces during the first year of the war. By the time Krol was given command of No. 302 Squadron at Northolt he had been credited with nine confirmed kills, although he did not add to his score whilst serving at Northolt.

When No. 317 Squadron arrived at Northolt it was commanded by Squadron Leader Kazimierz Rutkowski, although he handed over command to Squadron Leader Wlodzimierz Miksa in January 1944. The three Polish squadrons initially flew a mix of patrols and escort missions but then commenced bombing training during early 1944.

On 14 January 1944 No. 308 Squadron was providing fighter escort to Mitchell bombers detailed to attack targets in the Pas de Calais. As the formation was passing to the south-east of St Omer, they were attacked by a large formation of Focke-Wulf FW190s and

King George VI at Northolt during an official visit to the station in May 1944. The Typhoon pictured had flown in to Northolt and was one of a number of different types being inspected by the King prior to the D-Day operations.

during the following combat one of the Spitfires was shot down; the pilot, Flight Lieutenant Jan Piotrowski, was killed.

As the Allied invasion was now drawing nearer, the squadrons based furthest from the Channel were moved to bases along the south coast. Therefore, on 1 April Northolt was no longer designated No. 131 Airfield (this designation was moved to Chailey) and these were the last fighter squadrons to operate from Northolt. The three Polish fighter squadrons were replaced at Northolt by three more squadrons, which all operated different types in different roles. On 7 April Nos 16 and 140 Squadrons arrived from Hartfordbridge. Both squadrons were reconnaissance squadrons; No. 16 Squadron was equipped with Spitfire IXs and XIs and No. 140 Squadron was equipped with Mosquito IXs and XVIs. A month later No. 69 Squadron arrived at Northolt from the Mediterranean, having based at Luqa in Malta since January 1941. This squadron was equipped with Wellington XIIIs for night reconnaissance duties.

On 3 May the station received a visit from King George VI. By then all three Northolt squadrons were involved in reconnaissance missions during the final preparations for the Allied invasion of Europe. On D-Day, low cloud over the landing beaches meant that No. 16 Squadron had the difficult task of low-level reconnaissance of the Normandy beachhead. One of the first Allied casualties of D-Day was the loss of a Mosquito of No. 140 Squadron, which was lost during the early hours of 6 June whilst carrying out a reconnaissance sortie in the Cambrai area.

Northolt was not only used as a reconnaissance base during the D-Day period but it was also being increasingly used by transport aircraft as Northolt was ideal for receiving wounded from across the Channel as the Allied casualties started to increase. At the beginning of September the three squadrons left Northolt, which meant there were no resident squadrons at the airfield. However, the number of transport aircraft movements continued to increase and, at its busiest, the airfield activity increased to between 5–7,000 movements a month. Northolt was also used by the USAAF during the latter months of 1944.

Several improvements were made to Northolt during the latter stages of the war, which included a runway extension and the construction of a new B-1 type hangar. When the Second World War was over, Northolt's location made it an ideal choice for London's main airport whilst the site of Heathrow was being reconstructed. Northolt was handed over to the Ministry of Civil Aviation and many European commercial air companies and airlines operated from there until it was handed back to the RAF in 1954.

Northolt has been used by transport aircraft ever since and has continued to provide VIP transportation as one of its main roles. Today it is still used by the RAF and Northolt is now the home of No. 32 Squadron, which operates a variety of aircraft including the BAe 125 and 146, and Squirrel helicopters and performs Royal and other VIP duties. Although the A40 Western Avenue passes along the southern part of the airfield there are no stopping points from which to observe the airfield or aircraft movements. Furthermore, as it is an active RAF airfield there is no public access without prior permission.

Northolt's connection with the Second World War, and in particular with the Polish personnel who operated from there, is marked by the Polish War Memorial, which is located just outside the airfield's southern boundary. It can be accessed from a slip road off the A40 Western Avenue. More than 1,200 Polish airmen are commemorated on the memorial, including twenty-nine killed during the Battle of Britain. The memorial is constructed of stone, surmounted by a bronze eagle, and was unveiled on 2 November 1948. On the back is inscribed 'I have fought a good fight, I have finished my course, I have kept the faith'. The entrance to RAF Northolt can be found by turning left off the A40, when heading towards London, at the Polish War Memorial towards Northwood. The entrance is about 400 yards on the left.

Squadron	Dates at Northolt	Aircraft Type
302 Squadron	21 Sep 43 – 1 Apr 44	Spitfire IX
308 Squadron	29 Oct 43 – 1 Apr 44	Spitfire IX
317 Squadron	21 Sep 43 – 1 Apr 44	Spitfire IX
16 Squadron	7 Apr – 4 Sep 44	Spitfire IX & XI
140 Squadron	7 Apr – 3 Sep 44	Mosquito IX & XVI
69 Squadron	5 May – 4 Sep 44	Wellington XIII

The Polish Air Force Memorial at Northolt can be found alongside the A40 Western Avenue when heading towards London.

CHAPTER 5

Airfields of Kent

It is easy to understand why Kent has a close connection with aviation when considering its geographic position in the south-east of England and its close proximity to London. Kent's history of aviation dates back at least 120 years when the Army's School of Engineering was established at Chatham. From then on the area was used for various experiments in military aerial reconnaissance using balloons in the early days and later powered aircraft.

During the First World War many aircraft crossed the Channel to France from small landing grounds around Dover. As the war progressed more and more landing grounds were required, which is where the origins of some of the airfields in the south-east began. The formation of the RAF in 1918 meant that the airfields of Kent came under the command and control of No. 1 Area but many airfields and landing grounds disappeared at the end of the war only to be requisitioned or developed at the beginning of the Second World War.

The airfields of Kent will probably be best remembered for the Battle of Britain; indeed, five of the six featured in this chapter were heavily involved during the summer of 1940. Since then the names of Detling, Gravesend, Lympne, Manston and West Malling have all become familiar to aviation enthusiasts. But what is not always known is that these five airfields, plus Biggin Hill already covered in the previous chapter, went on to play important roles throughout the rest of the Second World War; in particular during the preparations for the Allied invasion of Europe. The sixth airfield covered in this chapter, Newchurch, was technically an Advanced Landing Ground rather than an airfield.

It is worth noting that there were several other landing grounds

developed in Kent during 1942 and 1943 but those that remained
inactive or in reserve, such as Swingfield, Brenzett, Lydd and New
Romney, are not included. Also not included are those landing
grounds handed to the US Ninth Air Force during the winter of
1943–4 and, therefore, under American command and control
during the period building up to and during the D-Day operations.
These include Ashford, Headcorn, High Halden, Kingsnorth,
Lashenden, Staplehurst and Woodchurch.

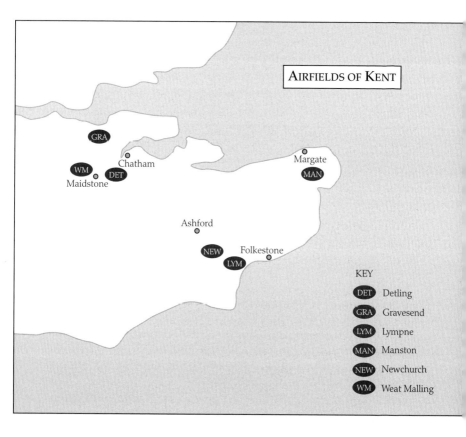

Detling

Detling dates back to the First World War and the site is now better known as the Kent County Showground. Following the formation of 2nd TAF in 1943 Detling was No. 125 Airfield of No. 83 Group and was home to Spitfire squadrons of No. 15 Wing during early 1944. On D-Day three squadrons of Spitfire IXs operated from Detling in support of the Allied invasion.

Now known to the public as the Kent County Showground, this former site was once an active airfield and was particularly busy during 1944 when the airfield was home to many RAF squadrons. Situated just to the north-east of Maidstone, Detling airfield dates back to 1915 when the site was first used by the Royal Naval Air Service and the Royal Flying Corps during the First World War. After the war the land reverted to farmland until the 1930s when it was redeveloped as an airfield as part of the RAF's Expansion Scheme.

Detling was initially used by Bomber Command but was then transferred to Coastal Command in 1938. The airfield was actively used during operations over France in the spring of 1940 and again during the Battle of Britain when it was home to Ansons of No. 500 Squadron and Blenheims of No. 53 Squadron. Even though Detling remained a Coastal Command airfield during the Battle of Britain, German intelligence considered it important enough to include it amongst their priority targets during the many raids on Fighter Command's airfields on 13 August 1940. The raid against Detling caused considerable damage to the runways and hangars, and more than twenty aircraft were destroyed on the ground. Sadly, more than sixty station personnel were killed, including the station commander, Group Captain Edward Davis, who was killed when the operations room received a direct hit.

There were further attacks against Detling before the Battle of Britain came to an end. With the raids over, there was much to be done to replace the damaged buildings and hangars. For the next two years Detling was home to various units before it transferred to Army Cooperation Command at the beginning of 1943 and then to Fighter Command in June. Detling then became No. 125 Airfield and No. 15 Wing moved in from Newchurch on 12 October.

Detling then came under the control of No. 83 Group, 2nd TAF, on 15 November. No. 15 Wing consisted of two squadrons of Spitfire IXs and one squadron of Hurricane IVs. The two Spitfire squadrons were No. 602 Squadron, under the command of Squadron Leader R.A. Sutherland, and No. 132 Squadron, under the command of Squadron Leader Franz Colloredo-Mansfeld. The son of an Austrian count and countess, Franz Ferdinand Colloredo-Mansfeld had left the USA to join the RAF soon after the outbreak of the Second World War and first served with No. 72 Squadron during 1942. He then served as a flight commander with No. 611 Squadron before being given command of No. 132 Squadron in August 1943.

The Hurricane squadron was No. 184 Squadron under the command of Squadron Leader Jack Rose, a veteran of the Battle of Britain. No. 184 Squadron was just one of three squadrons operating the Hurricane IV in the UK. The Hurricane IV could be armed with either two 40-mm cannons or fitted to carry 500-lb bombs or rocket projectiles depending on the mission. Although it was a very rugged aircraft, the Mk IV was not as popular amongst many pilots compared with other Hurricane variants. Because of the Mk IV's excess weight, it was less manoeuvrable than earlier variants and it had little or no speed advantage.

During the late morning of 21 December the Detling Spitfires were carrying a fighter sweep over the Cambrai area when they claimed a number of successes following an engagement with some forty Focke-Wulf FW190s. During the fierce air combat that followed, the Spitfires shot down three FW190s and claimed a further three as 'probably' destroyed. However, one pilot from each of the Detling squadrons was killed.

Leading the wing at Detling was twenty-three-year-old Wing Commander Robert Yule, a New Zealander and also a veteran of the Battle of Britain. Born in 1920, Robert Yule was awarded a scholarship at the RAF College Cranwell at the age of eighteen. His training course was cut short by the outbreak of the war and he was posted to No. 145 Squadron and saw considerable action during the battle over France and during the Battle of Britain. By the time he arrived at Detling in command of the wing, Robert Yule had been awarded the DFC and bar for the destruction of eight enemy aircraft and for his successful command of No. 66 Squadron. He was soon to add to his total on 7 January 1944 when he destroyed a FW190 over the Cambrai-Albert area, the scene of such devastation during the First World War. Soon afterwards Yule was awarded the DSO and he was then posted to No. 83 Group Headquarters, where he was involved in the planning and preparation for the forthcoming Allied invasion of Europe.

Another Detling pilot who enjoyed success during the same air combat was Flight Lieutenant Harry Walmsley of No. 132 Squadron who shot down a Focke-Wulf FW190 to the east of Abbeville; this was Walmsley's second confirmed kill, although he would go on to be credited with eleven kills by the end of the war. A week after Robert Yule was adding to his tally, Squadron Leader Franz Colloredo-Mansfeld was killed whilst returning to Detling at low-level across the French coast. He was leading the squadron when at about midday his Spitfire was shot down near Berck. Whether or not Colleredo-Mansfeld was shot down by an enemy fighter or by flak is unclear but it was, nonetheless, a tragic blow to the squadron and to Detling. At the time of his death he was thirty-three years old and he is buried in the Boulogne Eastern Cemetery.

During the same action, however, there was some success for twenty-three-year-old Flight Lieutenant Ken Charney of No. 602 Squadron who shot down a Focke-Wulf FW190 over St Pol; it was his fourth victory of the war. Three days later, following a recent period of intense air activity, Nos 132 and 602 Squadrons were rested from operations; both squadrons went north to Scotland for a well earned rest.

By early 1944 No. 184 Squadron had began its conversion to the Typhoon I and would eventually replace all its Hurricanes with the new type by March. The two Spitfire squadrons had worked tirelessly throughout December 1943 and early January 1944 and were heavily involved in fighter sweeps and fighter escort missions across the Channel, often encountering large numbers of enemy fighters. On 18 January they left Detling for Scotland and effectively changed bases with Nos 118 and 453 RAAF Squadrons; No. 132 Squadron moved to Castletown and No. 602 Squadron to Skeabrae.

It was not long before the two squadrons would return to Detling but in the meantime the two new squadrons quickly settled in, taking over the Spitfire IXs left at Detling by the two previous occupants. No. 118 Squadron was commanded by Squadron Leader Philip Heppell. The son of a First World War Royal Flying Corps pilot and known to his friends as 'Nip', Heppell was from Newcastle. He had joined the RAF following the outbreak of the war and had initially served with No. 616 Squadron, claiming his first two victories during the summer of 1941. He was awarded the DFC and then served in Malta with No. 249 Squadron during 1942, adding two more kills to his total. He then commanded No. 229 Squadron in Malta but was wounded in May 1943 and returned to the UK. After making a recovery 'Nip' Heppell took command of No. 118 Squadron at Detling in January 1944.

No. 184 Squadron lost one of its Hurricanes on 8 February when it was shot down over Zudausque; the pilot was killed. No. 453 Squadron RAAF flew its first operational sorties with 2nd TAF on 11 February when the squadron provided fighter escort for B-26s; all the Spitfires returned safely having had a quiet mission. The squadron then continued to fly mainly *Ramrod* missions across the Channel before, in April, it was also time for them to move on once more; this time, though, the journey was short to nearby Ford. No. 184 Squadron also left Detling at this same time; having completed its conversion to Typhoons, the squadron moved out to Odiham.

On 10 March No. 118 Squadron's personnel found themselves making the long journey back to Scotland and to Skeabrae. After their brief respite in Scotland, Detling's two original Spitfire squadrons returned once more; No. 132 Squadron arriving back on 11 March and No. 602 Squadron returning the following day. The squadrons were soon busy preparing for the forthcoming invasion of Europe, as well as taking part in attacks against V-1 sites across the Channel. The squadrons' association with Detling was short-lived second time round and both squadrons moved to Ford on 18 April.

As the Allied invasion was now drawing nearer, the squadrons based furthest from the Channel were moved to bases along the south coast and No. 125 Airfield moved from Detling to Ford. There was then a short period with no resident squadrons at Detling before a wing of three Spitfire IX squadrons arrived from Hornchurch on 19 May. The three squadrons were Nos 80, 229 and 274 Squadrons, all under the command of ADGB rather than 2nd TAF. The wing operated from Detling during the final build up to D-Day and during the invasion itself, mainly in the fighter-bomber role carrying out armed reconnaissance sorties across the Channel as well as fighter escort and sweep missions.

No. 80 Squadron had previously spent the war operating overseas in the North African and Mediterranean theatres. The squadron had moved literally dozens of times and its stay at Detling was to be typically short. In temporary command of the squadron during their short stay at Detling was Major Bjorn Björnstad, a Norwegian who had joined the RAF after escaping Norway following the German occupation. Björnstad had made his mark during 1943 whilst operating with No. 331 Squadron, the first of the Norwegian fighter squadrons in the RAF. He scored five victories during the year and was awarded the DFC before he was posted to No. 80 Squadron as a flight commander. On 14 June, whilst operating from Detling, Björnstad damaged a Bf109 during fighting over Beauvais in France.

No. 229 Squadron had also spent the war operating overseas, spending much of its time in Malta. Having returned to the UK in April 1944, the squadron took part in the build up to Operation *Overlord*. On D-Day itself, the squadron flew a mix of roles. Its early sorties were flown as escort to the invasion fleet and later in the day the squadron escorted the waves of gliders being towed across the Channel. Finally, late in the day, the squadron flew as bomber escort.

The third squadron at Detling during the D-Day period was No. 274 Squadron, another unit that had just returned from overseas. During the period it operated from Detling, the squadron was commanded by the Canadian 'Eddie' Edwards. One of the most distinguished pilots to have flown from Detling during the war, Edwards had already been credited with the destruction of fifteen enemy aircraft by the time he arrived at Detling, the majority of which had been whilst flying Kittyhawks with No. 260 Squadron in North Africa. He had scored considerable success during November 1942 when in addition to his aerial successes, Edwards destroyed a further eight *Luftwaffe* aircraft on the ground during attacks on airfields at Fuka, Gambut, Gazala and Marawa. By February 1943 Edwards had been awarded the DFM and DFC, and he celebrated his twenty-third birthday whilst at Detling. During June 1944 'Eddie' Edwards led many successful patrols over the Normandy beaches as well as numerous bomber escort missions, which later brought him the award of a bar to his DFC.

On 22 June, after just four weeks at Detling, all three squadrons moved out to Merston. Within weeks Nos 80 and 274 Squadrons would cross the Channel to support the final advance into Germany, although No. 229 Squadron remained at home before disbanding early in 1945. The two new squadrons to arrive at Detling were Nos 1 and 165 Squadrons, although this was to be a short stay of three weeks as both squadrons soon left for nearby Lympne; both squadrons, however, would return to Detling a month later.

The resident squadrons in between were Nos 504 and 118 Squadrons, which arrived on 11 and 12 July respectively, and No. 124 Squadron, which arrived on 26 July. The number of operational sorties being flown by the squadrons was continuously increasing. An example is No. 504 Squadron, which flew nearly 600 hours in July and nearly 650 hours during August 1944. No. 118 Squadron was still under the command of Squadron Leader 'Nip' Heppell and flew most sorties escorting bombers on their way to attack V-1 sites in Europe.

Spitfires of No. 132 Squadron during a formal inspection at Detling during early 1944.

On 10 August Nos 1 and 165 Squadrons returned from Lympne and both squadrons were to remain at Detling until the end of the year. No. 1 Squadron was commanded by Squadron Leader Pat Lardner-Burke. Born in South Africa, Lardner-Burke took command of the squadron in April 1944 after a short period at HQ Fighter Command. Lardner-Burke had led a charmed life after narrowly escaping death in November 1941 whilst operating in Malta with No. 126 Squadron. A bullet from an Aermacchi MC200 had penetrated his armour-plated seat, passed through his chest and punctured a lung. Despite his desperate wound, he managed to land safely back at Malta. After making a sufficient recovery, Lardner-Burke returned to England. He was awarded the DFC for the destruction of five enemy aircraft and took up instructional duties before returning to operational flying a year later. He then served as a flight commander with No. 222 Squadron during which time he added two more kills to his total. Pat Lardner-Burke commanded No. 1 Squadron throughout both periods at Detling and left the squadron at the end of 1944 having been awarded a bar to his DFC.

During the late summer and autumn of 1944 both Detling squadrons were involved in anti-Diver patrols to shoot down V-1 flying bombs inbound towards London as well as providing fighter escort missions. In September No. 165 Squadron provided fighter escort for the tugs and gliders taking part in Operation *Market*. Commanding No. 165 Squadron during the last few weeks at Detling was Squadron Leader Jas Storrar who had made his mark during the Battles of France and Britain during 1940. Storrar was just eighteen years old when he scored his first victory over France in May 1940 and was an ace with five victories before his nineteenth birthday. Four weeks after his nineteenth birthday came the announcement of the award of a DFC after scoring his eighth victory. By the time he took up command of No. 165 Squadron at Detling, Jas Storrar had been credited with at least twelve confirmed kills plus several more unconfirmed or officially described as 'probably destroyed'or 'shared'; he had also been awarded a well earned bar to his DFC.

The combination of Detling being a grass airfield and the rapid Allied advance into Germany meant that there was no further need for Detling as an operational station. Both squadrons moved out in mid-December 1944 and the airfield was placed on care and

The former airfield at Detling is now the Kent County Showground. The concrete pillbox on the right provides evidence that the site was once used for another purpose and marks the perimeter of the former airfield.

maintenance. No. 1 Squadron moved to Manston, where it would spend the rest of the war flying long-range fighter escort missions for Bomber Command, and No. 165 Squadron moved to Bentwaters, where it converted to the Mustang.

With the war over, Detling was transferred to No. 60 Group and a Signals Wing briefly moved in during the period 1946–7. The airfield was then used for gliding for the next ten years, although there was a brief period when Austers of No. 1903 Flight operated from the site during 1955 in support of the Army. Detling was reduced to care and maintenance in 1956, although Kent Gliding Club continued to use the airfield for a short while, and finally closed in 1959. The land was then taken over by Kent County Council and the site was used as the Agricultural Ground and then the Kent County Showground. There are a few visible reminders of its days as an airfield, such as the concrete pillboxes that mark the perimeter of the former airfield. The site can be found by taking the A249 from Junction 7 of the M20 at Maidstone, towards Sheerness. After just over 2 miles, the site of the former airfield is on the left and public access to the site is possible.

Squadron	Dates at Detling	Aircraft Type
132 Squadron	12 Oct 1943 – 17 Jan 1944	Spitifre IX
602 Squadron	12 Oct 1943 – 18 Jan 1944	Spitfire IX
184 Squadron	12 Oct 1943 – 6 Mar 1944	Hurricane IV & Typhoon I
118 Squadron	20 Jan – 10 Mar 1944	Spitfire IX
453 Squadron RAAF	19 Jan – 18 Apr 1944	Spitfire IX
132 Squadron	11 Mar – 18 Apr 1944	Spitifre IX
602 Squadron	12 Mar – 18 Apr 1944	Spitfire IX
80 Squadron	19 May – 22 Jun 1944	Spitfire IX
229 Squadron	19 May – 22 Jun 1944	Spitfire IX
274 Squadron	19 May – 22 Jun 1944	Spitfire IX
1 Squadron	22 Jun – 11 Jul 1944	Spitfire IX
165 Squadron	22 Jun – 13 Jul 1944	Spitfire IX
504 Squadron	11 Jul – 13 Aug 1944	Spitfire IX
118 Squadron	12 Jul – 9 Aug 1944	Spitfire IX
124 Squadron	26 Jul – 9 Aug 1944	Spitfire IX
1 Squadron	10 Aug – 18 Dec 1944	Spitfire IX
165 Squadron	10 Aug – 16 Dec 1944	Spitfire IX

Gravesend

First used by the RAF in 1933, Gravesend was used by 2nd TAF as No. 122 Airfield within No. 83 Group and was home to Spitfires and Mustangs of No. 15 Wing during early 1944. On D-Day the airfield was home to three Mosquito squadrons, which took part in fighter-bomber and night intruder missions in support of the Allied landings. Flying ceased from Gravesend in 1956 and the site is now the Riverview Park housing estate.

To the east of Gravesend in Kent, the Riverview Park housing estate now dominates the site where this former wartime airfield once stood. Gravesend dates back to the early 1930s when the increased popularity of flying, and the expansion of commercial aviation, led to the development of the airfield. The land chosen to the south of Chalk village and to the east of the town of Gravesend was some 250 feet above sea level and generally remained clear of fog, which made it an obvious and most suitable site for flying.

Although Croydon rapidly became London's main centre for aviation, Gravesend quickly established itself as an alternative site on the eastern side of the city and was home to several aircraft and commercial companies during the 1930s. The RAF first made use of the site in 1933 during exercises. When the Second World War began Gravesend was taken over by the Air Ministry and was used as a satellite airfield for Biggin Hill. During the Battle of Britain the airfield was initially home to Blenheims of No. 604 Squadron and then, from late July 1940, it was home to Hurricanes of No. 501 Squadron. During the early days of the battle, the Hurricanes would often deploy at first light to the forward operating airfield at Hawkinge and then return to Gravesend in the evening. However, an increasing number of air attacks against the airfields of Fighter Command soon meant that the squadron had to operate totally out of Gravesend.

Many famous fighter pilots flew from Gravesend during the Battle of Britain and the RAF's top scoring pilot during the battle, Sergeant 'Ginger' Lacey, scored nine of his eventual twenty-eight victories whilst serving with No. 501 Squadron at Gravesend. On 10 September the Hurricanes moved to Kenley and were replaced by Spitfires of No. 66 Squadron. This brought another young pilot to the fore, twenty-one-year-old Flight Lieutenant Bobby Oxspring, who destroyed eight enemy aircraft whilst operating from Gravesend during September and October. These are just two names of many fine young men who flew from Gravesend during the Battle of Britain and this period marks an enormously important part of the airfield's history.

The facilities at Gravesend were not the best during 1940, which is one of the main reasons why only one squadron operated from the airfield at any one time. With the battle over, however, the facilities were soon improved and Gravesend became a fully functioning station. Between 1942 and 1943 the size of the airfield was increased to accommodate two lengthened runways; the east–west runway was increased to 1,800 yards and the north–south runway to 1,700 yards. Sommerfield track was also laid to help ensure all-year round operations.

By 1943 the runways had been lengthened and the airfield buildings and facilities improved so that three squadrons could operate from the airfield at any one time. Between April and September 1943 eleven different fighter squadrons consisting of Typhoons, Spitfires and Mustangs, all passed through Gravesend; some only stayed a few days, others only stayed a few weeks. The situation settled down at the end of October when Nos 19, 65 and 122 Squadrons were in residence; these three squadrons would remain at Gravesend until April 1944 under the command and control of No. 83 Group, 2nd TAF.

Commanding No. 122 Squadron at Gravesend, and later the wing, was Squadron Leader Pete Wickham. A graduate of the RAF College Cranwell, Wickham had first flown Gladiators whilst detached to No. 33 Squadron in the Middle East during 1940. He then served in Greece, flying Hurricanes, and then commanded No. 111 Squadron Spitfires; Wickham was awarded the DFC and bar after taking his total to nine kills.

From 19 November 1943 No. 65 Squadron was commanded by Squadron Leader Reg Grant. Born in New Zealand, Grant had joined the RNZAF and travelled to the UK at the beginning of the Second World War. By the time he arrived at Gravesend he had personally been credited with seven kills, for which he had been awarded the DFC and bar to add to the DFM he had received in 1941 as a sergeant pilot.

Up until this time No. 122 Airfield Wing had been led by Wing Commander Harold Bird-Wilson. One of the RAF's outstanding young fighter pilots, Bird-Wilson had made his mark during the Battles of France and Britain during 1940. He was just twenty-three years old when he led the wing at Gravesend and had just been awarded a bar to his DFC when he handed over command to Wing Commander Pete Wickham on 3 December. Bird-Wilson was subsequently rested from operations, although he would later return to operations during the summer of 1944.

One key date for 2nd TAF during December 1943 was the 22nd when the first Mustang III aircraft was delivered to No. 65 Squadron – the first unit to take delivery of the RAF's variant of the American P-51B Mustang. The most noticeable difference between the RAF's variant and that of the American Air Force was the canopy design; the Mustang III had a framed canopy with a side-hinge, which differed from the blister canopy found on the P-51B. It was not long before the other two squadrons at Gravesend took delivery of the Mustang III to complete the RAF's first Mustang wing.

The three Gravesend squadrons began working up with Mustangs early in 1944. Although No. 65 Squadron had taken delivery of its first Mustangs, the squadron also continued to fly its Spitfire IXs on operations. On 3 January 1944 two of its aircraft failed to return from a *Ranger* sortie in the Brussels area; one of the pilots was killed with the other taken as a prisoner of war. On 6 January Gravesend's Spitfires carried out a fighter escort mission for medium bombers of No. 2 Group detailed to attack 'Noball' targets. The formation was attacked and the Gravesend Spitfires became involved in a fierce dogfight, which resulted in one Focke-Wulf FW190 being shot down.

On 8 January Wing Commander Pete Wickham completed his tour of operations and he handed over command of No. 122 Airfield to Wing Commander Reg Grant who in turn handed over command of No. 65 Squadron to Squadron Leader 'Robin' Johnston. Born in South Africa, Johnston was educated in England where he had joined the Cambridge University Air Squadron. Commissioned into the RAF Volunteer Reserve just before the outbreak of the Second World War, Johnston had initially served in the Middle East where he enjoyed considerable success whilst flying Hurricanes with No. 73 Squadron during 1942; he was appointed as a flight commander and then took command of the squadron before being awarded the DFC after his fourth victory. He returned to the UK in January 1944 when he was given command of No. 65 Squadron at Gravesend.

No. 19 Squadron flew its last operational sorties with Spitfires on 24 January 1944, after which it would operate the Mustang III. Its Spitfire Mk IXs, incidentally, were passed to the Canadian squadrons at Kenley. Both Nos 19 and 65 Squadrons commenced operations with the new Mustang on 15 February. On 28 February Gravesend suffered a tragic loss when Wing Commander Reg Grant was killed whilst taking off to lead the wing on a *Ramrod* mission. It is believed that his Mustang suffered a major engine failure and Grant crashed some 3 miles to the east of the airfield. Reg Grant was twenty-nine years old at the time of his death. It was, indeed, a tragic blow for all at Gravesend. Command of the wing was then passed to Wing Commander 'Robin' Johnston who was promoted having not long been in command of No. 65 Squadron. During the next two months Johnston would lead the wing with distinction. Many of the wing's sorties involved daylight fighter escort for American bombers during which Johnston was able to increase his personal score to nine confirmed kills for which he would be awarded the DSO and a bar to his DFC.

Mustangs of No. 19 Squadron, which served at Gravesend during the period February to April 1944.

In turn, command of No. 65 Squadron was given to Squadron Leader 'Jerry' Westenra. Born in Christchurch, New Zealand, 'Jerry' Westenra had joined the RNZAF in 1940 and then travelled to the UK later that year. He had previously served in the Middle East with No. 112 Squadron, initially flying Gladiators in Greece and then flying Tomahawks and Kittyhawks in the Western Desert. He was awarded the DFC in 1942 and would go on to lead No. 65 Squadron with distinction throughout the D-Day operations, after which he would be awarded a bar to his DFC.

There were other changes in command at Gravesend. Squadron Leader Mac Gimour took command of No. 19 Squadron and Squadron Leader Ian Morrin took command of No. 122 Squadron. The increased range of the Mustang meant that the squadron's new role would include long-range fighter escort as well as dive-bombing targets in northern France and armed reconnaissance. As the date of the Allied invasion drew closer, the squadrons based furthest from the Channel were moved to bases along the south coast and on 15 April all three squadrons of No. 122 Airfield moved from Gravesend to Ford.

Two days later Mosquitos of No. 21 Squadron, No. 464 Squadron RAAF and No. 487 Squadron RNZAF moved into Gravesend from Hunsdon. The squadrons were all equipped with the Mk VI variant and were involved in fighter-bomber operations by day and intruder missions at night; the squadrons often carried out precision daylight attacks against specific targets. This was the Mosquito Wing that carried out the famous daylight raid against the prison at Amiens just two months earlier to relieve French prisoners awaiting certain death at the hands of the *Gestapo*.

The three Mosquito squadrons remained at Gravesend throughout the period leading up to, and including D-Day. Their targets included bridges, rail junctions, road junctions and targets of opportunity moving towards the invasion area. No. 464 Squadron RAAF lost one of its Mosquito aircraft during an intruder mission in the early hours of 3 June when it came down near Laon; the crew were both killed.

After the Allied landings the squadron continued a mix of daylight and night intruder missions before leaving Gravesend for Thorney Island on 18 June; all three squadrons would later cross the Channel to operate from the European mainland.

The launch of the V-1 attacks against London during the summer

The Cascades Leisure Centre on the Riverview Park estate provides a landmark to the site of the former airfield at Gravesend.

of 1944 brought an end to flying operations at Gravesend; the airfield became surrounded by barrage balloons and it was simply considered too hazardous getting in and out of Gravesend.

At the end of the war Gravesend was placed on care and maintenance. The Essex Aero Company used the site until the mid-1950s but the airfield was eventually closed for flying in 1956. The land was then sold by the Air Ministry and the construction of a large housing estate began before the decade was out. Today the housing estate dominates the site and there are no obvious signs of the former airfield. In addition to the Riverview Park estate there is also a golf course and sports complex. In the entrance to the Cascades Leisure Centre there is a plaque proudly displayed to commemorate the fifteen pilots killed whilst serving at Gravesend during the Battle of Britain. The site of the former airfield can be found by taking the A2 from the M25 towards Rochester. Continue past the Gravesend turn-off and about 2 miles before the A2 becomes the M2, take the road off to the left to the village of Thong. After about 3 miles, and having passed through the village, the golf course can be seen on the right and the housing estate on the left. This marks the area of the former airfield. The turning into the Leisure Centre is on the right.

Squadron	Dates at Gravesend	Aircraft Type
277 Squadron	7 Dec 42 – 15 Apr 44	Various Air-Sea Rescue
174 Squadron	5 Apr – 12 Jun 43	Typhoon I
247 Squadron	28 May – 4 Jun 43	Typhoon I
19 Squadron	20 – 26 Jun 43	Spitfire V
132 Squadron	20 Jun – 2 Jul 43	Spitfire
V 4 Squadron	16 Jul – 7 Aug 43	Mustang I
2 Squadron	16 Jul – 10 Aug 43	Mustang I
306 'Torunski' Squadron	11 – 19 Aug 43	Spitfire V
257 Squadron	12 Aug – 17 Sep 43	Typhoon I
193 Squadron	17 Aug – 18 Sep 43	Typhoon I
64 Squadron	19 Aug – 6 Sep 43	Spitfire V
266 Squadron	7 – 10 Sep 43	Typhoon I
19 Squadron	24 Oct 43 – 15 Apr 44	Spitfire IX & Mustang III
65 Squadron	24 Oct 43 – 15 Apr 44	Spitfire IX & Mustang III
122 Squadron	3 Nov 43 – 15 Apr 44	Spitfire IX & Mustang III
21 Squadron	17 Apr – 18 Jun 44	Mosquito VI
464 Squadron RAAF	17 Apr – 18 Jun 44	Mosquito VI
487 Squadron RNZAF	17 Apr – 18 Jun 44	Mosquito VI

2

Pen & Sword Books
FREEPOST SF5
47 Church Street
BARNSLEY
South Yorkshire
S70 2BR

DISCOVER MORE ABOUT MILITARY HISTORY

Pen & Sword Books have over 1500 titles in print covering all aspects of military history on land, sea and air. If you would like to receive more information and special offers on your preferred interests from time to time along with our standard catalogue, please complete your areas of interest below and return this card (no stamp required in the UK). Alternatively, register online at www.pen-and-sword.co.uk. Thank you.

PLEASE NOTE: We do not sell data information to any third party companies

Mr/Mrs/Ms/Other........................Name...

Address...

....Postcode.......................

Email address...
If you wish to receive our email newsletter, please tick here ❒

PLEASE SELECT YOUR AREAS OF INTEREST

Ancient History ❒	Medieval History ❒	English Civil War ❒
Napoleonic ❒	Pre World War One ❒	World War One ❒
World War Two ❒	Post World War Two ❒	Falklands ❒
Aviation ❒	Maritime ❒	Battlefield Guides ❒
Regimental History ❒	Military Reference ❒	Military Biography ❒

Website: www.pen-and-sword.co.uk • Email: enquiries@pen-and-sword.co.uk
Telephone: 01226 734555 • Fax: 01226 734438

Lympne

Another Kent airfield with its origins dating back to the First World War, Lympne was used on D-Day by three squadrons of Spitfires under the command and control of No. 11 Group ADGB. The site later became Ashford Airport in the 1960s but the land is now an industrial park and a wild animal park.

Situated about 3 miles to the west of the village of West Hythe, some 7 miles to the west of Folkestone in Kent, is the former airfield of Lympne. The origins of the airfield date back to the First World War when the site was first used as an emergency landing ground for home defence units of the Royal Flying Corps. After the war the site was used for civil aviation during the 1920s, although the RAF always maintained an interest in the site and Lympne was occasionally used by auxiliary squadrons during the late 1920s.

During the build up to the Second World War Lympne was increasingly used by the RAF. In 1939 the airfield was placed under the command and control of Fighter Command but there were initially no resident squadrons, although many squadrons did use the airfield when returning across the Channel during the Battle of France. During the Battle of Britain Lympne was used as a forward operating airfield for squadrons of No. 11 Group. As a result the airfield came under attack from the *Luftwaffe*. The first attack took place on 12 August 1940 and resulted in the destruction of six hangars as well as other administrative and technical buildings. Further attacks later that week effectively put the airfield out of action for the following few weeks, although Lympne was still used for emergency landings.

Lympne was not used operationally again until the spring of 1941 when squadrons operated from the airfield whilst conducting fighter sweeps across the Channel. Gradually the facilities were upgraded so that the airfield could accommodate two squadrons at the same time. Lympne played a vital role in providing air cover for assaulting forces against the port of Dieppe on 19 August 1942, when Spitfires of No. 133 Squadron deployed forward from Gravesend and No. 401 Squadron RCAF deployed from Biggin Hill to operate from Lympne on the day.

The facilities at Lympne were then further upgraded so that the airfield could accommodate a third squadron. Although hangars and buildings were built at Lympne, the runway remained grass, the longest being just 1,400 yards in length. This always meant that operating in and out of Lympne was tight to say the least. The mainstay squadron at Lympne from the spring of 1943 was No. 1 Squadron, equipped with Typhoons, which arrived from Biggin Hill on 15 March. The squadron would remain at Lympne for nearly a year, which was quite unusual for that period of the war when fighter squadrons were regularly moved around the south of England.

When No. 1 Squadron arrived at Lympne it was commanded by Squadron Leader 'Wilkie' Wilkinson, a veteran of the Battle of France. During the battle he had gained considerable success as a sergeant pilot; he was awarded the DFM and bar for his nine victories during the campaign. He was later commissioned and had commanded No. 174 Squadron during 1942 but was shot down over France. Having evaded capture, Wilkinson eventually made his way back to the UK and was given command of No. 1 Squadron at Acklington in August 1942 as the squadron was preparing to convert to the Typhoon. Whilst at Lympne the Typhoons of No. 1 Squadron mainly took part in daylight *Rhubarbs*, anti-shipping attacks and fighter escort missions, although it would later take part in bombing attacks against enemy airfields and V-1 sites across the Channel in northern France.

In May 1943, command of No. 1 Squadron was handed over to Squadron Leader Zweigburgh and he would remain in command for the squadron's remaining time at Lympne, On 18 August Typhoons of No. 609 Squadron moved to Lympne from Matlask under the command of Squadron Leader Pat Thornton-Brown. Ten days after arriving at Lympne, Thornton-Brown scored his first victory of the war when he shot down a Focke-Wulf FW190 to the south of Verneuil. No. 609 Squadron remained at Lympne until 14 December when it moved to Manston. Sadly, Pat Thornton-Brown was killed just a week after the move when he was shot down over Doullens whilst escorting American bombers of the US Eighth Air Force.

Changing place with the Typhoons of No. 609 Squadron at Lympne were Hurricanes of No. 137 Squadron from Manston, which arrived at Lympne on the same day that No. 609 Squadron departed for Manston. The Hurricanes were rocket-armed Mk IVs and the squadron mainly took part in anti-shipping strikes. No. 137 Squadron briefly left Lympne for Colerne at the beginning of 1944 to convert to the Typhoon and then returned to Lympne on 4 February 1944 to undertake fighter-bomber sorties. When the Typhoons of No. 137 Squadron returned to Lympne, they were still part of No. 11 Group and would not officially join 2nd TAF until later in the summer; they were the last Typhoon unit to transfer to 2nd TAF. No. 1 Squadron left Lympne for Martlesham Heath on 15 February. Two weeks later Spitfires on No. 186 Squadron arrived from Tain, although the Spitfires would only remain at Lympne for a month. No. 137 Squadron also left Lympne at the beginning of April.

The airfield then became home to a wing of three squadrons for the first time when Spitfire IXs of the North Weald Wing arrived at Lympne on 17 May. The wing was under the command and control of ADGB and consisted of Nos 33, 74 and 127 Squadrons. No. 74 Squadron was commanded by Squadron Leader James Hayter from New Zealand who had been awarded the DFC in 1941 whilst serving with No. 611 Squadron and had assumed command of No. 74 Squadron in Iran earlier in 1943. Hayter had taken the squadron to Egypt before returning to the UK to take part in the Allied invasion of Normandy.

Spitfire of No. 403 Squadron RCAF at Lympne during the early weeks of 1944.

Typhoon I of No. 137 Squadron at Lympne. The squadron had converted from the Hurricane IV during the period January to February 1944.

Although the facilities at Lympne had been improved throughout the war, they were still no match for those that the squadron pilots and ground crew had left behind at North Weald. The Lympne Wing flew the first of many sweeps on 19 May. The wing was led by Wing Commander Ray Harries, a Welshman and former medical student. By the time Harries had been appointed as a wing leader, he had been awarded the DSO and the DFC and two bars for his outstanding leadership and for having taken his personal tally to fourteen confirmed kills.

The Lympne Wing carried out several fighter sweeps across the Channel during the final preparations for the invasion of Europe and during the period immediately after. Weather permitting, operations usually began at first daylight and continued through to dusk and sometimes beyond into the early night. On D-Day itself the squadrons took part in beachhead patrols and escorted gliders across the Channel to the invasion area, although the day proved relatively uneventful.

As the Allies started to breakout of the Normandy area, the squadrons found themselves on the move once more. On 3 July the wing moved to Tangmere on transfer to 2nd TAF and was replaced at Lympne by a Czech Wing consisting of Nos 310, 312 and 313 Squadrons. However, these three Czech squadrons remained at Lympne for just a week before moving out to go their separate ways. The Czech squadrons were replaced by Spitfires of No. 41

Squadron and by No. 1 Squadron who returned to Lympne once more. The third squadron to take up residency was No. 165 Squadron. The three Spitfire squadrons at Lympne became increasingly involved in anti-Diver patrols to counter the V-1 threat to London but as the threat reduced, the two Mk IX squadrons moved out to Detling in August.

No. 41 Squadron was then joined at Lympne by No. 130 Squadron and then No. 610 Squadron. Both these squadrons were also equipped with powerful Spitfire XIVs and the three squadrons formed a Mk XIV Wing to counter the new Messerschmitt Me262 jet fighters, which were continuously harassing the American bombers taking part in daylight bombing raids over Europe. In September No. 130 Squadron was replaced by No. 350 'Belgian' Squadron. The wing continued to fly fighter sweeps and bomber escort missions until December when the three squadrons moved across the Channel to operate from mainland Europe. Lympne was then used as an emergency airfield until the end of the war.

At the end of the Second World War Lympne was placed on care and maintenance before it was then used for commercial purposes for flights to France and Belgium. The airfield was renamed Ashford Airport in 1968 and the facilities further improved.

The best view of the old buildings and across the former airfield at Lympne is from the B2067 next to the Lympne Industrial Park and before reaching the Wild Animal Park.

However, a decline in commercial airfreight across the Channel,
and the larger development of other airfields in the south of
England resulted in the gradual demise of the airport during the
1970s. Flying eventually ceased and the site was then developed
into what is now Lympne Industrial Park. Port Lympne, which was
once the location of the Officers' Mess, is now part of Port Lympne
Wild Animal Park and Gardens.

The site of the former airfield can be found near Junction 11 of the
M20. From there take the A20 towards Ashford, past Folkestone
Race Course and then turn left along the B2067; this is signposted to
the Wild Animal Park. The industrial park is soon found on the left.
The industrial park and land to the south of the B2067, about 3 miles
to the west of the village of West Hythe, is the area of the former
airfield, although evidence has all but disappeared.

Squadron	Dates at Lympne	Aircraft Type
1 Squadron	15 Mar 43 – 15 Feb 44	Typhoon I
609 Squadron	18 Aug – 14 Dec 43	Typhoon I
137 Squadron	14 Dec 43 – 2 Jan 44	Hurricane IV
	4 Feb 44 – 1 Apr 44	Typhoon I
186 Squadron	1 Mar – 5 Apr 44	Spitfire V
33 Squadron	17 May – 3 Jul 44	Spitfire IX
74 Squadron	17 May – 3 Jul 44	Spitfire IX
127 Squadron	17 May – 4 Jul 44	Spitfire IX
310 'Czech' Squadron	3 – 11 Jul 44	Spitfire IX
312 'Czech' Squadron	4 – 11 Jul 44	Spitfire IX
313 'Czech' Squadron	4 – 11 Jul 44	Spitfire IX
1 Squadron	11 Jul – 10 Aug 44	Spitfire IX
41 Squadron	11 Jul – 5 Dec 44	Spitfire XIV
165 Squadron	13 Jul – 10 Aug 44	Spitfire IX
130 Squadron	11 Aug – 30 Sep 44	Spitfire XIV
610 Squadron	12 Sep – 4 Dec 44	Spitfire XIV
350 'Belgian' Squadron	29 Sep – 3 Dec 44	Spitfire XIV

Manston

Another Kent airfield under the command and control of No. 11
Group ADGB on D-Day was Manston, which operated Typhoons
and Mosquitos in support of the Allied invasion of Europe. This
famous site was first used for flying during the First World War and
is now Kent International Airport.

Now the vast site of Kent International Airport, this once famous
wartime airfield was right in the front line of Fighter Command's
defences during the Battle of Britain. Located 2 miles to the west of
Ramsgate on the Isle of Thanet the airfield is easily found. Its
origins date back to the First World War when the German Zeppelin
airships first appeared in the sky over southern England during
1915. This meant that more airfields were needed in south-east
England and Manston was developed during 1916 for use by the
Royal Naval Air Service. A hangar and other permanent buildings
were constructed and the site was then used during 1917 by one of
two main RNAS flying instructional units, the other being at
Cranwell in Lincolnshire.

After the First World War there was an inevitable reduction in
flying activity from Manston, although the site was retained by the
post-war RAF. Manston's many buildings and large area made the
site ideal for technical training and in 1919 the School of Technical
Training moved to Manston from Halton. In 1921 flying activity
resumed from the airfield and Manston was used for pilot refresher
training for pilots destined for deployment overseas. During the
mid-1930s Manston was home to the RAF's School of Air
Navigation and No. 3 Technical Training School. The RAF's
expansion during the latter years of the 1930s saw both training
schools move out and Manston was transferred to Fighter
Command soon after the outbreak of the Second World War.

During the spring of 1940 the airfield was used by many
squadrons involved with providing fighter cover across the
Channel in support of ground forces in France and also during the
evacuation of Dunkirk. Like many other RAF fighter airfields, the
Battle of Britain took a major place in the history of Manston. Its
location made it ideal for use as a forward operating airfield for No.
11 Group and many squadrons spent time deployed to Manston
during the early phase of the battle. At that time the airfield was

grass and up to three squadrons at a time could deploy flights of fighters to Manston during daylight hours before returning to their home bases at night. The only resident squadron at Manston during the Battle of Britain was No. 600 Squadron, which operated Blenheims from the airfield between June and August 1940.

The fact that Fighter Command was using Manston as a forward operating airfield and because of its close proximity to German forces based in northern France, meant that Manston became an obvious target for the *Luftwaffe*. Soon after midday on 12 August the airfield received a devastating attack by Messerschmitt Bf110s, resulting in significant damage to the airfield, hangars and buildings. Such was the damage that German intelligence believed the airfield was knocked out of action but the efforts of those at Manston meant that it was back ready for action again the following day. Two days later the same happened again; on this occasion the attack was even more devastating than before. Three Blenheims were completely destroyed on the ground and four hangars were badly damaged.

The low-level attacks continued daily thereafter, causing more damage and casualties. It is indeed great credit to the personnel of Manston that the airfield remained operational throughout much of this devastation but the fact was that Manston could not continue to sustain such devastating attacks. The situation became desperate on 24 August by which time there were no communications with the Sector Airfield at Hornchurch and there was little or no water for much of the time. In addition to the damage on the ground, there had been heavy losses in the air. One section of Defiants of No. 264 Squadron based at Hornchurch was on the ground at Manston for refuelling when an attack took place. There was little warning for the Defiant crews and as they tried in vain to get airborne three were shot down immediately and one was shot down within a few minutes as it tried to get away; seven of the aircrew were killed. The devastation caused as a result of these continuous attacks meant that the Blenheims of No. 600 Squadron were withdrawn and operations from the airfield temporarily ceased, although Manston did resume operations in early September.

After the Battle of Britain, Manston was used by a number of different squadrons during 1941. In February 1942 Manston was used by the Fleet Air Arm during its heroic attempt to stop the German battleships *Gneisenau* and *Scharnhorst* breaking out of the

French port at Brest and passing through the Dover Straits. Manston was then used by the North Weald Wing for fighter operations across the Channel and the airfield was also used as an emergency landing site for Bomber Command and American bombers of the US Eighth Air Force.

On 19 August Manston was used by four Spitfire squadrons during the famous Dieppe Raid: No. 242 Squadron, Nos 331 and 332 (Norwegian) Squadrons, and No. 403 RCAF Squadron. The two Norwegian squadrons and No. 242 Squadron had deployed forward to Manston from their home base at North Weald on 14 August; the Canadians had deployed south from their base at Catterick. During the action of 19 August the wing was led by Wing Commander David Scott-Malden who, at the age of just twenty-three years old, had commanded the North Weald Wing since March 1942. The aerial fighting over Dieppe was fierce. No. 332 (Norwegian) Squadron and No. 403 RCAF Squadron both enjoyed some success but they had also suffered particularly badly. The two Norwegian squadrons were caught up in the heaviest fighting of the day. Although they claimed thirteen enemy aircraft destroyed between them, No. 332 (Norwegian) Squadron lost four Spitfires during the air action with two more damaged; fortunately, no pilots had been killed but two were lost as prisoners of war and one was wounded. The Canadians were also heavily involved and claimed five successes but lost three Spitfires; all three pilots were killed. The day following the Dieppe Raid, 20 August, the North Weald Wing returned home and the Canadians returned to Catterick.

In April 1943 the airfield was used by Barnes Wallis for trials of his famous bouncing bomb during preparations for the raid on the German dams. In June work began to extend Manston's main runway to 3,000 yards and a large perimeter loop, with crash bays, was also constructed. On 11 June Typhoons of No. 3 Squadron moved to Manston from West Malling and the following day Hurricane IVs of No. 184 Squadron arrived from Merston. In July, another Typhoon squadron, No. 56 Squadron, arrived from Matlask but only remained at Manston a month before moving to Bradwell Bay where it exchanged places with another Typhoon squadron; No. 198 Squadron arrived at Manston on 23 August. Also in August, two more Hurricane IV squadrons arrived: No. 164 Squadron from Warmwell and No. 137 Squadron from Southend.

It was indeed a very busy period at Manston with Hurricane IVs

Typhoons operated with No. 137 Squadron at Manston during the D-Day operations. Shown here armed with rocket projectiles, the Typhoon was capable of attacking and destroying a variety of targets.

and Typhoon Is operating from the airfield together. The Hurricane IV could carry 500-lb bombs or rocket projectiles (RPs). The rocket installation was fitted under the wings and a rocket armed Mk IV weighed about 1,000 lbs more than a standard Hurricane. Generally, four 60-lb rockets were mounted under each wing on long rails with a protective plate located under the leading edge to protect the wing from cordite blast. Whilst at Manston, No. 184 Squadron was equipped with both RP Mk IV and cannon-armed Mk IID Hurricanes so that it could choose which type was best for any given task. For example, the Mk IIDs could be typically employed against trains or vehicles in occupied France and the Mk IVs could be used against shipping in the Channel.

The various movements in and out of Manston meant that by the end of September 1943 three squadrons remained: one Hurricane IV squadron, No. 137 Squadron, and two Typhoon fighter-bomber squadrons, No. 3 Squadron and No. 198 Squadron, and it remained this way until mid-December 1943. The Typhoons of No. 198 Squadron were initially under the command of Squadron Leader Mike Bryan who had been awarded the DFC in March 1943 for his outstanding contribution to fighter-bomber operations and, in particular, for the destruction of twenty railway engines. In November Mike Bryan handed over command of the squadron to Squadron Leader Johnny Baldwin, although Mike Bryan would later return to command the squadron again in April 1944.

At twenty-five years old, Johnny Baldwin had joined the RAFVR as an airman at the outbreak of the Second World War. He initially served as ground crew in France and then on bomb disposal duties during the London Blitz of 1940. Having volunteered for pilot training in 1941, Baldwin had rapidly progressed through the commissioned ranks to take over command of No. 198 Squadron in November 1943; he had also been awarded the DFC after being credited with shooting down three Bf109s in a single action over Dover on 20 January 1943.

The Typhoons were continually involved in operations across the Channel, often taking part in fighter escort missions deep into occupied Europe. No. 137 Squadron continued to carry out a variety of sorties until December when it started preparations to convert to the Typhoon. By then a detachment of Wellington XIIIs of No. 415 Squadron RCAF had arrived at Manston, as had Spitfire VIs of No. 1401 (Met) Flight, which had been moved to Manston to conduct weather reconnaissance sorties over Europe; this flight would remain at Manston for the duration of the D-Day operations.

In February 1944 the Typhoons of No. 3 Squadron returned to Manston once more to join the remaining two Typhoon squadrons, Nos 198 and 609 Squadrons, to briefly form the Typhoon wing of No. 123 Airfield under the command of No. 84 Group, 2nd TAF. This was short-lived, however, as the change of squadrons and airfields continued and all three Typhoon squadrons had left Manston by the end of March; No. 3 Squadron moved to Bradwell Bay and Nos 198 and 609 Squadrons moved to Tangmere.

On 15 March Typhoons of No. 183 Squadron arrived from Tangmere. Although the squadron remained at Manston for just two weeks, it was not an easy time. Six days after arriving, Flight Lieutenant Peter Raw, one of the flight commanders, was killed on a *Ranger* sortie having been shot down by ground defences whilst carrying out an attack at low-level against enemy barges on the River Waal. Raw was an experienced Typhoon pilot and was a tragic loss to the squadron.

As the Allied invasion drew nearer, No. 123 Airfield moved from Manston to Thorney Island on 1 April. No. 183 Squadron was replaced by the Typhoons of No. 137 Squadron, which returned to Manston once more. A week later No. 605 Squadron, equipped with Mosquito VIs, arrived from Bradwell Bay to carry out night intruder operations across the Channel. On 23 May Beaufighters of No. 143 Squadron arrived from North Coates to carry out anti-E Boat patrols in the Channel, along with Fleet Air Arm units, as part of No. 16 Group Coastal Command; the detachment of Wellingtons of No. 415 Squadron RCAF had moved out in mid-April. Manston was also being increasingly used as a main diversion airfield, its location making it an ideal first landing point for bombers returning back from Europe.

During the final run-up to the Allied invasion of Europe, and on D-Day itself, there was much activity at Manston. On 9 May more than twenty Typhoons of No. 124 Wing arrived from Hurn to take part in a long-range fighter sweep mission in the areas over Knocke, Rheims and Grandvilliers. Manston's resident squadrons were continually involved on operations: the Mosquitos of No. 605 Squadron were tasked with attacking enemy airfields and anti-aircraft installations; the Beaufighters of No. 143 Squadron were involved in anti-shipping in the Channel; and the Typhoons of No. 137 Squadron provided support to the Army on the ground. At the same time the Spitfire VIs of No. 1401 (Met) Flight continued with vital weather reconnaissance missions across the landing beaches and northern France.

In July two more, and very different, units took up residence at Manston. No. 119 Squadron re-formed at Manston on 19 July with Albacores, which were used for anti-shipping patrols at night, and two days later the first Meteor jet fighters of No. 616 Squadron arrived from Culmhead. Manston was then used by fighters carrying out anti-Diver patrols, looking for V-1s, and the airfield was also used during the airborne operations over Arnhem and Nijmegen during September. Otherwise, there were continuous movements of various fighter squadrons and wings in and out of Manston for the rest of the war.

After the Second World War Fighter Command considered there

was no further use for Manston and the airfield transferred to Transport Command in 1946. From 1950 the airfield was used by the Americans. In 1956 Manston's large runway and facilities resulted in it gaining the status of a Master Diversion Airfield for use in emergencies; this meant the requirement to remain open twenty-four hours a day, every day of the year.

Manston was used by many different military and civilian units and organisations during the 1960s and 1970s. In particular it was home to RAF Search and Rescue helicopters from 1961 until the station of RAF Manston closed in 1999. However, the civilian-operated part of the airfield remained and the site became Kent International Airport. Today the airfield dominates the Isle of Thanet and can easily be found by taking the A229 and then the A259 towards Ramsgate and then following the signs. The runway itself is situated between the A259 and B2190; the A259 follows the line of the old southern taxiway close to the main runway and the B2190 cuts across the site of the old RAF station. There are some original buildings left, including the southernmost hangar on the western side, which was there during the Battle of Britain, and an original black hangar building dating back to 1918; this is situated near the original site of the old watch office.

The Allied Aircrew Memorial in front of the Spitfire and Hurricane Memorial Building at Manston.

Looking across to the south-east and the air traffic control tower.

By following the B2190 around the northern side of the runway, you will pass through the main site and there is much of historical interest to be found. The Spitfire and Hurricane Memorial Building was first opened in June 1981 and the adjoining part of the building was opened in October 1988. Outside the building is the Allied Aircrew Memorial, which was unveiled by Her Majesty Queen Elizabeth the Queen Mother on 18 July 1997. There is also the Allied Air Forces Memorial Garden overlooking the main airfield. No charge is made for admission but as it is totally self-funding then donations are always most welcome. The members of staff are volunteers and are always most helpful. There is free car parking and refreshments available at the Merlin Cafeteria. There is also provision for wheel chair access. The Memorial Building is open throughout the year with the exception of three days during the Christmas period and also New Year's Day. Opening times are from 10.00 a.m. to 5.00 p.m. from April to September, and from 10.00 a.m. to 4.00 p.m. from October to March. The address is: The Spitfire and Hurricane Memorial Building, Manston, Ramsgate, Kent, CT12 5DF. The Memorial Building is signposted from the A259.

At the same location is the RAF Manston History Museum; this is next to the Memorial Building and is open daily. Further along the road, on the left opposite the Air Traffic Control tower, is the MoD's Defence Fire Training and Development Centre.

Squadron	Dates at Manston	Aircraft Type
3 Squadron	11 Jun – 28 Dec 43	Typhoon I
184 Squadron	12 Jun – 14 Aug 43	Hurricane II & IV
56 Squadron	22 Jul – 23 Aug 43	Typhoon I
164 Squadron	5 Aug – 22 Sep 43	Hurricane IV
137 Squadron	8 Aug – 14 Dec 43	Hurricane IV
198 Squadron	23 Aug 43 – 17 Mar 44	Typhoon I
415 Squadron RCAF (detachment)	15 Nov 43 – 29 Apr 44	Wellington XIII
609 Squadron	14 Dec 43 – 16 Mar 44	Typhoon I
3 Squadron	14 Feb – 6 Mar 44	Typhoon I
1401 (Met) Flt	Nov 43 – Jan 45	Spitfire VI
183 Squadron	15 Mar – 1 Apr 44	Typhoon I
137 Squadron	1 Apr – 13 Aug 44	Typhoon I
605 Squadron	7 Apr – 21 Nov 44	Mosquito VI
143 Squadron	23 May – 9 Sep 44	Beaufighter X
119 Squadron	19 Jul – 9 Aug 44	Albacore I
616 Squadron	21 Jul 44 – 17 Jan 45	Meteor I

Newchurch

Developed only for flying operations during the Second World War,
Newchurch was an Advanced Landing Ground within No. 85
Group, 2nd TAF, and was home to Tempests and Spitfires of No. 150
Wing during the D-Day operations. The land has long reverted to
agriculture.

Situated 5 miles to the south of Ashford in Kent, the airfield of
Newchurch was another Advanced Landing Ground developed in
the south-east of England and was only used during the latter half
of the Second World War. The site was first identified during 1942
and land was developed to the west of the village of Newchurch, on
the northern edge of Romney Marsh.

The airfield was completed by the spring of 1943. There were two
Sommerfield tracks laid, which gave Newchurch two runways for
use; one in a north–south direction and the other east–west.
Newchurch became part of the newly formed No. 125 Airfield
structure with very basic facilities, although two blister hangars
were later built. Personnel were accommodated in tents, although
some local billeting also took place. The first flying units to arrive at
Newchurch were Spitfire Vs of Nos 19 and 132 Squadrons, which
both arrived on 2 July 1943 from Bognor and Gravesend
respectively.

No. 19 Squadron was led at Newchurch by Squadron Leader
Victor Ekins, a former chartered surveyor and veteran of the Battle
of Britain. Awarded the DFC, Ekins had been given command of
No. 19 Squadron in November 1942. Leading No. 132 Squadron at
Newchurch was the Austrian Squadron Leader Franz Colloredo-
Mansfeld, who had travelled from the USA following the outbreak
of the Second World War to serve with the RAF. Another holder of
the DFC, Colloredo-Mansfeld had previously served with No. 72
Squadron and then as a flight commander with No. 611 Squadron
before being given the command of No. 132 Squadron soon after the
squadron moved to Newchurch.

These two squadrons operated together during the summer of
1943, mainly providing fighter escort for American daylight
bombing missions over occupied Europe. On 13 August No. 19
Squadron was replaced by No. 602 Squadron, which arrived from
Kingsnorth and was led by Squadron Leader Mike Beytagh. Born in

China, Beytagh was brought up in the USA and joined the RAF in 1936. He flew Hurricanes with No. 73 Squadron during the Battle of Britain and then flew in the North African theatre with the same squadron before returning to the UK at the end of 1941. He was given command of No. 602 Squadron in October 1942 and soon after was awarded the DFC; his citation stated five victories. Whilst operating from Newchurch, Mike Beytagh made his final claim of the war; damage to a FW190 over Amiens on 19 August.

The two Spitfire squadrons at Newchurch were joined by Hurricanes of No. 184 Squadron on 17 September, commanded by Squadron Leader Jack Rose. The Hurricanes had arrived from Snailwell and the squadron was in the process of replacing cannon-armed Mk IIs with rocket-capable Mk IVs. Its main role whilst at Newchurch was a mix of attacks against enemy shipping in the Channel and operations against selected ground targets in northern France. Jack Rose had served with Nos 3 and 32 Squadrons during the Battle of Britain and was awarded the DFC in October 1942; he was then given command of No. 184 Squadron when it formed at Colerne in December 1942.

On 12 October 1943, No. 125 Airfield moved to Detling. Newchurch then closed to operations as the airfield was further developed and improved. The development included the construction of two additional hangars and improved taxiways. In April 1944 Newchurch re-opened as No. 150 Airfield under the command and control of No. 85 Group, 2nd TAF, in preparation for receiving three Tempest squadrons. The first of these, No. 3 Squadron, moved in from Bradwell Bay on 28 April. The same day No. 56 Squadron moved south from Ayr, although it would be a few weeks before this squadron took delivery of the Tempest; in the meantime it operated a mix of Spitfires and Typhoons. The following day, Tempests of No. 486 Squadron RNZAF, arrived from Castle Camps.

The three squadrons were dispersed around the airfield. No. 3 Squadron was situated at the north-eastern corner of the airfield. No. 56 Squadron was on the western boundary and No. 486 Squadron RNZAF towards the south-western corner of the airfield. Commanding No. 3 Squadron at Newchurch was Squadron Leader Allan Dredge. Having served as a sergeant pilot with No. 253 Squadron during the Battle of Britain, Dredge was commissioned in March 1941. He then served with No. 261 Squadron during the defence of Malta before being shot down in May 1941 and badly burned. Eventually returning to the UK he was admitted to the Victoria Hospital before returning to operations in 1943. He served with No. 183 Squadron and was awarded the DFC before he assumed command of No. 3 Squadron in October 1943.

On 12 May 1944 there was a restructuring within 2nd TAF, which saw the bigger fighter wings become Sectors and the Airfields, which had previously been numbered, became Wings using the corresponding number previously allocated. Newchurch became No. 150 Wing under the command and control of No. 25 Sector within No. 85 Group.

The three Newchurch squadrons of No. 150 Wing were led by the legendary pilot, Wing Commander Roland 'Bea' Beamont. At the time he led No. 150 Wing from Newchurch, Beamont was still only twenty-three years old. Although his moderate academic ability

The legendary pilot Roland Beamont who led the Newchurch Wing during the D-Day air operations at the age of just twenty-three.

meant that he did not enter the RAF College Cranwell, he instead entered the RAF on a short service commission and quickly proved to be an exceptional pilot. During the Battle of France he flew Hurricanes with No. 87 Squadron and claimed his first success on 13 May 1940 – a Dornier Do17 over Belgium. Awarded the DFC in 1941, Beamont was then court-martialled for taking a WAAF flying in his Hurricane! Fortunately, he got away with a warning. He then flew as a test pilot with the Hawker Aircraft Company and this was to be the start of his exceptional career in test flying. The experience he gained flying the Typhoon at Hawker meant that he was at the forefront of Typhoon operations and tactics in the RAF. He flew Typhoons with No. 56 Squadron and then No. 609 Squadron, taking command of this squadron in October 1942. He was awarded a bar to his DFC in January 1943, which was followed by the DSO in May. He then returned to Hawker for a rest from operations once more where he flew the Tempest. In March 1944 he was promoted to the rank of wing commander and took command of the Castle Camps Wing before moving to Newchurch as Officer Commanding No. 150 Wing within 2nd TAF. Two days after D-Day, on 8 June, Beamont achieved his first success for nearly two years when he shot down a Bf109 to the west of Rouen. Bea Beamont was awarded a bar to his DSO in July. Whilst commanding the wing during the V-1 attacks against London, Beamont was credited with shooting down thirty V-1 flying bombs. During operations over Europe in October 1944 he was shot down and taken prisoner of war. After the war Bea Beamont became a test pilot with Gloster and then he was appointed as Chief Test Pilot for English Electric. His impressive career as a test pilot included flying the prototype Canberra, the Lightning, the TSR2 and the Tornado; Bea Beamont eventually retired in 1979.

The two Tempest squadrons of No. 150 Wing were vital assets of 2nd TAF during the build up to D-Day and had now commenced operations with their new type. The squadrons were both involved in shipping reconnaissance and air-ground strafe of key targets in northern France. On 27 May two Tempests of No. 3 Squadron failed to return from a shipping reconnaissance mission along the northern coast of the Pas de Calais, although the circumstances behind the losses are unknown. There was, however, success for the squadron just four days later when Wing Commander Beamont led a flight of Tempests from the squadron on a *Rodeo* across France during which the pilots destroyed four Junkers Ju88s on the ground.

For the Tempests of No. 150 Wing, D-Day proved relatively quiet but the days that followed proved busy as the Allies started to break out of the Normandy beachhead. When the Germans mounted their V-1 attacks against London, the wing became involved in daylight and night patrols in an attempt to shoot down the V-1s. To help the wing with the night patrols, the Fighter Interception Unit (FIU) moved to Newchurch during July. The top scoring V-1 ace was Squadron Leader Joe Berry who served with the FIU at Newchurch during this period. Flying the Tempest V, Berry was eventually credited with the destruction of an incredible fifty-nine V-1s, all achieved during the three-month period between the end of June and September 1944 for which he was awarded the DFC and bar. Sadly, Joe Berry was killed during low-level operations over Germany on 2 October 1944 when his aircraft was hit by flak and he crashed in flames; a second bar to his DFC was later announced.

No. 150 Wing left Newchurch for Matlask during September 1944. The first unit to leave was No. 486 Squadron RNZAF on 19

Having long reverted to agriculture, there remains little, if any, evidence that this was the site of Newchurch during 1944. The farm in the right of the picture is Oak Farm and the area this side of the farm is where No. 56 Squadron operated from during the D-Day operations.

September, followed by No. 3 Squadron two days later and, finally, No. 56 Squadron on 23 September. The airfield facilities were slowly removed and the airfield closed in 1945.

Today there remains very few, if any, reminders of this once busy and active airfield. The village of Newchurch can be found by taking the A207 south from Ashford. After about 7 miles, before reaching Brenzett Green, turn left on a minor road for about 5 miles across the northern edge of Romney Marsh towards Newchurch. The site of the former airfield can be gauged by the minor roads leading to farms to the west and north-west of the village of Newchurch, which once formed the boundary of the site. The three minor roads lead to Oak Farm, Brooker Farm and Wills Farm. Just to the north of Oak Farm is the northern edge of the airfield. No. 56 Squadron operated from just south of the farm during the D-Day period and the wing HQ was also located in this part of the airfield, as were the tents for the squadron's ground crew. To the south-west of Wills Farm is the south-western corner of the airfield; No. 486 Squadron RNZAF operated from just in front of the farm. Just to the west of Brooker Farm was the bulk fuel installation.

Squadron	Dates at Newchurch	Aircraft Type
19 Squadron	2 Jul – 18 Aug 43	Spitfire V
132 Squadron	2 Jul – 12 Oct 43	Spitifre V
602 Squadron	13 Aug – 12 Oct 43	Spitfire V
184 Squadron	17 Sep – 12 Oct 43	Hurricane II & IV
3 Squadron	28 Apr – 21 Sep 44	Tempest V
486 Squadron RNZAF	29 Apr – 19 Sep 44	Tempest V
56 Squadron	28 Apr – 23 Sep 44	Spitfire IX, Typhoon I, Tempest V

West Malling

On D-Day West Malling was a 2nd TAF airfield and was home to Mosquitos and Spitfires of No. 148 Wing, No. 85 Group. After the war the airfield was used by jet fighter squadrons until the RAF moved out in 1967. Today the site is used by Kent County Council and is called King's Hill, named after the original landing ground used during the First World War.

Although the airfield of West Malling has long since gone, and the site re-developed, there do remain some reminders of this famous wartime airfield. Situated 7 miles to the north-west of Maidstone in Kent, West Malling was originally called King's Hill and was first used during the First World War as a relief landing ground for the Royal Flying Corps. It was not until 1930 that it was opened as an airfield and the site was initially used for private flying. The airfield became Maidstone Airport in 1932 and then the Malling Aero Club in 1935.

After the outbreak of the Second World War the airfield was taken over by the RAF. It was an all-grass airfield and West Malling was used during the Battle of Britain as a satellite airfield for Kenley and also as a second operating airfield for nearby Biggin Hill. The only resident squadron at West Malling during the opening days of the battle was No. 26 (Army Cooperation) Squadron, which operated Lysanders. On 12 July Defiants of No. 141 Squadron arrived at Malling, having moved south from their previous base at Turnhouse in Scotland. Just a week after arriving at Malling the squadron suffered a devastating blow. On 19 July the squadron's Defiants were engaged over the Channel by Bf109s of JG51. The aerial fighting that followed was bitter and, although the squadron claimed some success, six Defiants were shot down with the loss of ten men killed; this effectively wiped out No. 141 Squadron in just one single action and the squadron was posted back north just two days later.

There were several devastating air attacks against West Malling during August 1940, which left the airfield less effective for much of the battle. One attack took place at 7.30 a.m. on 10 August. The attack was at low-level and came without warning. Fourteen bombs fell inside the airfield's boundary and caused considerable damage to two aircraft on the ground and several buildings; one of the station's personnel died and many more were injured. There was a further attack just five days later, during the early evening; on this occasion the attack was made from medium-level and two of West Malling's personnel were killed. Within the next three days there were two further attacks; during the second of these three Lysanders were written off. By the first week in September there had been a further three attacks and these continual attacks resulted in significant damage to West Malling. Many buildings had been destroyed, communications to its chain of command had been lost and West Malling's personnel had been stretched to their limits; continually doing their best to repair the damage only to find all their hard work destroyed again a day or two later.

This period of intense attacks also led to the withdrawal of No. 26 (Army Cooperation) Squadron on 3 September. Furthermore, West Malling could not be used by any of Fighter Command's squadrons. This did not stop the attacks, however, and there were further losses to station personnel. Operations did eventually resume at Malling on the penultimate day of the Battle of Britain when Spitfires of No. 66 Squadron moved in on 30 October but it was not until the spring of 1941 that West Malling was restored to full operational status. It had been a devastating period in the airfield's history.

Improvements to the airfield continued during 1941, which involved the laying of Sommerfield track to give West Malling more capability in terms of poor weather operations. This gave the airfield four runways: the longest runway was 1,400 yards long and ran east to west (this runway would be lengthened further later on); the south-east to north-west runway was 1,300 yards; a north to south runway was 1,200 yards (this runway would also be lengthened later on); and the north-east to south-west runway was 1,100 yards.

During 1942 several squadrons operated from the airfield. During the famous Dieppe Raid of 19 August 1942, West Malling was host to three Spitfire squadrons: No. 411 Squadron under the command of Squadron Leader R.B. Newton; No. 485 Squadron under the command of Squadron Leader Reg Grant; and No. 610 Squadron under the command of the legendary Squadron Leader Johnnie Johnson. The day proved to be one of the greatest air battles of the war and ended with mixed fortunes for the West Malling squadrons. Between them they achieved some noticeable successes with at least four enemy aircraft destroyed and several more claimed. For example, Johnnie Johnson recorded his seventh kill of the war, a Focke-Wulf FW190 over the port of Dieppe, and he also shared in the destruction of a Messerschmitt Bf109. However, the squadrons had lost four pilots killed between them; the Canadians of No. 411 Squadron came off worst with two pilots killed and one more wounded.

There were more squadron movements in and out of West Malling during 1943. These included fighters of the US Air Force, which took part in bomber escort missions over Europe. In May 1943 No. 85 Squadron arrived at West Malling from Hunsdon. For the next year this Mosquito squadron operated from West Malling under the command of the legendary night-fighter ace Wing Commander John 'Cat's Eyes' Cunningham. John Cunningham was born in Croydon in July 1917. He was educated at the Whitgift School, Croydon and then attended the De Havilland Technical School in 1935. He joined No. 604 Squadron Auxiliary Air Force later that year and then became a test pilot with de Havilland in 1938. When the Second World War broke out, Cunningham was mobilised with his squadron. The squadron became fully employed as a night-fighter squadron during the summer of 1940 and then took delivery of its first Beaufighters. On the night of 19/20 November 1940 Cunningham claimed his first victory – a Junkers Ju88 he shot down north of Bridge Norton. A month later he added a second to his score and soon after Cunningham crewed up with radar operator Sergeant Jimmy Rawnsley. Together, this crew achieved notable success as a night-fighter crew with the squadron. During one night, 15/16 April 1941, the crew shot down three Heinkel He111s in one night. John Cunningham was given command of No. 85 Squadron in January 1943 and by the time he arrived at West Malling in May 1943 he had been credited with sixteen confirmed kills and several more claimed as damaged, all whilst flying Beaufighters; for this achievement Cunningham had been awarded the DSO and bar, and the DFC and bar.

Three days after the squadron arrived at West Malling it achieved a notable success when crews shot down four Focke-Wulf FW190s and claimed another as a probable. These were the first successes against the FW190 at night and all were over the UK. By then the squadron had also taken delivery of five night-fighter Mosquito XVs, which could operate up to 43,000 feet. Cunningham himself achieved his first kill in a Mosquito (a Mk XII variant) and his seventeenth kill overall, whilst operating from West Malling on the night of 13/14 June 1943; this was a FW190 over Wrotham.

During the period August and September 1943, four squadrons came and went from West Malling: Nos 130, 234, 64 and 350 (Belgian) Squadrons, all Spitfire V squadrons, all came and went in just a matter of a few weeks. The Canadian squadron, No. 410 Squadron RCAF which operated Mosquitos, arrived in October but departed just a month later. This left No. 85 Squadron as the only long-term resident squadron during this period of changes.

By early 1944 the No. 85 Squadron scoreboard recorded the squadron's two hundreth kill. John Cunningham had taken his personal total to twenty destroyed, which made him the RAF's highest scoring night-fighter pilot at the time. Cunningham was awarded a second bar to his DSO and he then left West Malling, handing over command of No. 85 Squadron to Wing Commander Charles Miller in March 1944. Charles Miller soon made his mark at West Malling, shooting down a Junkers Ju88 near Dymchurch on the night of 18/19 April. John Cunningham was promoted to the rank of group captain to take up his next appointment at HQ No. 11 Group. After the war Cunningham was released back to De Havilland where he continued to make history as the company's Chief Test Pilot; most notably he flew the first Comet airliner. He retired in 1980 and lived in Hertfordshire. John 'Cat's Eyes' Cunningham, one of the most famous pilots to have served at West Malling during the Second World War, died in 2002.

No. 85 Squadron had been joined at West Malling in September 1943 by No. 124 Squadron, which operated Spitfire VIIs. Whilst at West Malling No. 124 Squadron essentially operated two flights; one flight carried out fighter sweeps across the Channel whilst the second flight, a high-altitude flight, carried out its fighter operations at high-level. These mixed operations proved successful with the high-altitude claims typically being a handful a month. This pattern continued through the winter months but then changed slightly when the squadron became increasingly involved in providing fighter escort for RAF bombers. The squadron remained at West Malling until March 1944 when it moved north to Church Fenton in Yorkshire.

No. 124 Squadron was replaced by No. 616 Squadron under the command of Squadron Leader Les Watts but, like so many other fighter squadrons, this unit only remained at West Malling for a month. The third squadron to stay at West Malling for some months during this period was No. 96 Squadron, which operated Mosquito XIIIs. This squadron arrived at West Malling in November 1943 and was commanded by Wing Commander Edward Crew. Born in Northamptonshire in 1917, Crew had been educated at Cambridge before he joined the University Air Squadron. He was commissioned into the RAF Reserve soon after the outbreak of the Second World War and joined No. 604 Squadron in July 1940. He made his mark as a night-fighter pilot and was credited with his first kill on the night of 4/5 April 1941. By the end of July 1941 he was a night-fighter 'ace' and his most noticeable achievement was during the night of 7/8 July when he destroyed two enemy aircraft (a Junkers Ju88 and a Heinkel He111) over Southampton. More success followed in 1942 and he was given command of No. 96 Squadron in June 1943. By the time Edward Crew arrived at West Malling in November 1943, he had been credited with nine confirmed kills for which he had been awarded the DFC and bar. Whilst operating from West Malling, Edward Crew took his total to twelve: he shot down one Messerschmitt Me410 off Beachy Head during the night of 4/5 January 1944 (he also claimed another as damaged); he shot down a Ju188 over Whitstable on the night of 13/14 February; and destroyed another Me410 over Brighton on the night of 18/19 April.

No. 85 Squadron left West Malling on 1 May 1944 and was replaced by No. 29 Squadron, which also operated Mosquitos. By then No. 91 Squadron had replaced No. 616 Squadron (Spitfire VIIs) and soon after No. 409 Squadron RCAF arrived from Hunsdon. These changes meant that there were to be four squadrons operating out of West Malling during the final build up, and during, the D-Day operations of 6 June 1944: Nos 96, 29 and 409 RCAF Squadrons, all operating various marks of the Mosquito in the night-fighter role, and No. 91 Squadron with Spitfire XIVs.

On 12 May there was a re-structuring within 2nd TAF, which saw the bigger fighter wings become Sectors. Likewise, the Airfields, which had previously been numbered, became Wings using the corresponding number previously allocated. West Malling became No. 148 Wing and was tactically allocated to No. 24 Sector to operate alongside the Mosquito XIIIs of No. 147 Wing at Zeals, which was all under the command and control of No. 85 Group.

No. 29 Squadron flew its first intruder missions with Mosquito

XIIIs on 14 May and this was to be the squadron's main role whilst at West Malling during the D-Day period of operations. From 19 May the Spitfire XIVs of No. 91 Squadron were given approval to take part in offensive patrols over northern France. For the Canadians of No. 409 RCAF Squadron, the combination of its move south to Malling, and to 2nd TAF, and its re-equipment with Mosquitos, had reinvigorated the crews of the squadron; the squadron had spent the previous year in the north-east of England with very little operational activity. The crews of No. 409 RCAF Squadron quickly commenced training in intruder operations and the squadron soon scored its first victory for over a year.

During the D-Day operations No. 409 RCAF Squadron was flying patrols over the Normandy beaches. On 9 June the squadron destroyed a Ju188 and shot down three more enemy aircraft the following night. By the end of June the squadron had been credited with the destruction of eleven enemy aircraft for the loss of two

Unveiled in 2002, the memorial at the end of Gibson Drive at King's Hill stands as testament to those that served at West Malling.

crews. The squadron left West Malling in 19 June for Hunsdon.

With the Allied forces starting to break out of the Normandy beachhead, No. 96 Squadron became involved in anti-Diver patrols as the Germans launched its V-1 campaign against London in June. The squadron left West Malling for Ford on 20 June as the V-1 intensity increased and its squadron commander, Edward Crew, went on to eventually be credited with twenty-one V-1s destroyed.

By 20 June the three Mosquito squadrons had left West Malling. On the same day that the Mosquitos departed, No. 91 Squadron was joined by another Spitfire squadron, No. 322 (Dutch) Squadron. This squadron had formed in June 1943 with all-Dutch personnel. The squadron flew a mix of patrols along the south coast, escort missions for airborne forces and then anti-Diver patrols. The squadron only remained at West Malling for a month.

On 4 July Mustangs of No. 316 'Warszawski' Squadron arrived at West Malling but only remained a week before moving on to Friston. The following day two more Spitfire squadrons arrived at West Malling; this temporarily brought the number of fighter squadrons at West Malling to five. The two latest arrivals were Nos 80 and 274 Squadrons, equipped with Spitfire IXs, and both these squadrons remained at West Malling until the end of August. During this time No. 85 Squadron had returned to West Malling and No. 157 Squadron (Mosquito XIXs) had arrived from Swannington.

By the end of August 1944, the 'merry-go-round' of squadron movements in and out of West Malling had come to an end. The Allied advance towards Germany had gathered momentum and all the squadrons would, for the time being, be needed elsewhere. West Malling then closed for air operations as the airfield went through a major redevelopment programme. The airfield re-opened just as the war was coming to an end and was then used to receive prisoners of war returning to the UK once hostilities were over. West Malling then became home to various types of aircraft including the RAF's new jet fighter, the Meteor, and later the Javelin. In 1960 West Malling closed as an operational airfield and was placed on care and maintenance before the RAF finally moved out in 1967. The airfield was used briefly afterwards by the US Navy before the local council purchased the site in 1970 and converted its buildings into office accommodation.

The site of this famous wartime airfield covers more than 500 acres of land. It has been completely redeveloped and the area is now the location of Kent County Council's King's Hill council offices, business premises for a number of companies and a golf course; King's Hill being the original name of the airfield. However, some of the RAF buildings from the post-war period remain. A memorial was erected and unveiled on 9 June 2002 to mark the site of the airfield and it now stands as a testament to the military and civilian personnel who served at West Malling. It includes the names of some of the famous airmen who flew from the airfield during the Second World War: Wing Commander Peter Townsend, Wing Commander Bob Braham, Wing Commander John 'Cat's Eyes' Cunningham and Wing Commander Guy Gibson. Next to the memorial stands a statue of an unnamed airman with the crests of the squadrons that flew from the airfield during the war.

The site can be found outside the village of West Malling by taking the A228 from Junction 4 of the M20. Then continue along the A228, bypassing the village of West Malling, for about 3 miles until you see the King's Hill council complex on your left. Turn left and proceed along Gibson Drive as far as possible (about a mile), across

The former air traffic control tower still stands amongst the large redevelopment at King's Hill. It can be found in Queen's Street.

a large roundabout, and you will reach the memorial and statue. Also in the vicinity is the former air traffic control tower, which is worth going to see considering it has survived the major redevelopment in the area. It can be found by returning back down Gibson Drive, turning left at the roundabout into Forest Way and then taking the next left into Discovery Way. Continue along Discovery Way across a roundabout and then turn left into Fortune Way. Then take the next left into Queen's Street and the air traffic control tower is immediately on the right.

Squadron	Dates at West Malling	Aircraft Type
85 Squadron	13 May 43 – 1 May 44	Mosquito XII, XIII, XV & XVII
3 Squadron	14 May – 11 Jun 43	Typhoon I
130 Squadron	4 Aug – 18 Sep 43	Spitfire V
234 Squadron	5 Aug – 16 Sep 43	Spitfire V
64 Squadron	6 – 25 Sep 43	Spitfire V
350 (Belgian) Squadron	7 – 18 Sep 43	Spitfire V
124 Squadron	20 Sep 43 – 18 Mar 44	Spitfire VII
410 Squadron RCAF	22 Oct – 8 Nov 43	Mosquito XII
96 Squadron	8 Nov 43 – 20 Jun 44	Mosquito XIII
616 Squadron	18 Mar – 24 Apr 44	Spitfire VII
91 Squadron	23 Apr – 21 Jul 44	Spitfire XIV
29 Squadron	1 May – 19 Jun 44	Mosquito XII & XIII
409 Squadron RCAF	14 May – 19 Jun 44	Mosquito XIII
322 (Dutch) Squadron	20 Jun – 21 Jul 44	Spitfire XIV
316 'Warszawski' Squadron	4 – 11 Jul 44	Mustang III
80 Squadron	5 Jul – 29 Aug 44	Spitfire IX
274 Squadron	5 Jul – 17 Aug 44	Spitfire IX
85 Squadron	21 Jul 44 – 29 Aug 44	Mosquito XII
157 Squadron	21 Jul – 28 Aug 44	Mosquito XIX

CHAPTER 6

Airfields and Advanced Landing Grounds of Sussex

Only two of the six sites covered in this chapter were developed as airfields and both have survived to the present day. Gatwick and Shoreham airports need little, if any, introduction. However, the four other sites remain largely unknown to most except the real aviation enthusiast. Although the names of Chailey, Coolham, Deanland and Friston might be familiar to the local population of Sussex, it is almost certain that the majority will be unaware of what once happened at these quiet locations. In fact, all four of these sites were developed as Advanced Landing Grounds, or ALGs, rather than as airfields.

These ALGs were amongst a number of sites identified in the south during 1942 for possible use by single-engine fighters of Fighter Command during the planned invasion of mainland Europe. At that stage of the war it was not clear where the invasion would take place, although at that time it was thought it was likely to be in the Pas-de-Calais area. The sites identified as ALGs had to be ready by the spring of 1943, although poor weather meant that many were not completed until later in the year. The layout for all the ALGs was very much along the same plan; two Sommerfield track runways of some 1,000 yards or more in length and laid at approximately ninety degrees to each other. The Sommerfield track was essentially a runway of heavy steel netting held rigid by steel bars secured by pickets. The intention was that aircraft operations could only really be conducted during fair weather and never during the winter. During the period 1942–3 some plans changed, and other proposed sites were dropped. Understandably, there was strong opposition at the time to the Air Ministry's plans to convert countryside into airfields, most notably from the Ministry of Agriculture, and many of the proposed sites were not developed. However, in the end, a compromise was struck and only twenty-three of the sites were developed.

Essentially, the difference between ALGs and those sites that were given full airfield status was that the ALGs were never planned for permanent use and, therefore, were not constructed with any permanent buildings or features, either domestic or technical. They were, however, more than just bare fields in the countryside and they were given appropriate security protection. Furthermore, because construction generally started around the mid-1942 period and D-Day did not occur until two years later, many of these sites were quite well developed and 'homely' by the time they were no longer needed.

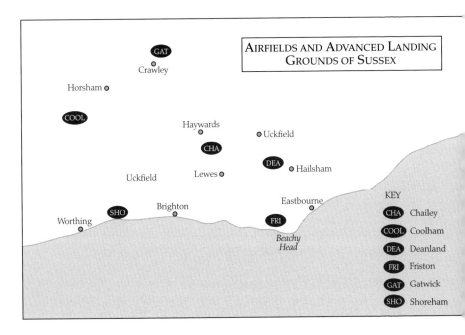

Chailey

With one of the shortest aviation histories, Chailey was an Advanced Landing Ground used by 2nd TAF and was home to three Polish Spitfire squadrons of No. 131 Wing, No. 84 Group, during the D-Day operations. After the war the land reverted to agriculture and is now the site of Bower Farm.

Chailey is amongst the least known of the airfields used by 2nd TAF during the D-Day air operations. It is situated in East Sussex about 4 miles to the south-east of Haywards Heath and to the east of Burgess Hill. The name Chailey is derived from the Saxon word *chag*, which was the name given to the gorse that grew in the area, although both the name and pronunciation have changed over the years. Geographically, Chailey lies either side of the A275 and is reputedly the centre of the County of Sussex. Furthermore, if you visit Lane End Common you will find the Meridian Stone, which marks the point where the Greenwich Meridian Line passes through the Parish of Chailey. Therefore, by standing at the stone you can have one foot in the western hemisphere and the other in the eastern.

The airfield of Chailey has one of the shortest histories. It was only in existence for about a year and was only used operationally for a matter of weeks either side of D-Day. However, for a few months in 1944 this quiet and very green part of East Sussex was home to many Polish personnel and three Polish squadrons of Spitfires. Not only did Chailey become an active airfield, the surrounding countryside was home to thousands of American and Canadian troops that were camped in the large wooded areas on the edge of the South Downs.

Although referred to as an airfield, Chailey was, in fact, an Advanced Landing Ground, or ALG, and was constructed during early 1943 on farmland near Plumpton Green in a dense wooded area marking the northern boundary of what is now the South Downs National Park. As with all ALGs, the facilities were extremely basic and no permanent domestic accommodation was ever built. The main runway was 1,500 yards orientated east–west. The second runway was 1,200 yards and ran from the south-east to the north-west. The runways were reached by taxiways from three basic aircraft dispersals. Four blister hangars were erected for basic technical servicing. As Chailey would only ever be used to provide short-term air support during the period of the Allied invasion of Europe, there was no need for any permanent domestic accommodation as the squadron personnel would be housed in tents. However, in reality, many local farms and cottages were requisitioned to supplement the basic accommodation.

Although complete by the winter of 1943 there was no immediate flying activity from Chailey and the land was released back to the farmers whilst the plans for D-Day materialised. Eventually, as D-Day approached, the first aircraft moved into Chailey, which was numbered as No. 131 Airfield as part of No. 84 Group, 2nd TAF. Three Polish Spitfire IX squadrons moved in from nearby Deanland on 26 April 1944. Both No. 302 Squadron and No. 308 Squadron had formed during the Battle of Britain; indeed, No. 302 Squadron had been the first Polish fighter squadron that formed in the UK during the Second World War. No. 317 Squadron, however, had formed in February 1941. The three Polish squadrons together formed No. 131 Wing within No. 84 Group.

Whilst at Chailey, No. 302 Squadron was commanded by the experienced Polish pilot, thirty-two-year-old Squadron Leader Marian Duryasz, a veteran of the Battle of Britain. Duryasz was born in Warsaw in 1911 and joined the Polish Air Force in 1932. After the German invasion of Poland at the outbreak of the Second World War Duryasz arrived in England in January 1940 and joined No. 213 Squadron at Exeter during the Battle of Britain. After the battle he was briefly posted away from the squadron but returned to operations in March 1941 when he was posted to No. 317 Squadron, back at Exeter, as a flight commander. After a period with No. 316 Squadron during 1943, Duryasz was posted to No. 302 Squadron in January 1944 and then took command of the squadron in June, just as the squadron moved to Chailey.

No. 308 Squadron was commanded at Chailey by Squadron Leader Witold Retinger. Having just celebrated his twenty-sixth birthday, Retinger was the youngest of the three squadron commanders. He was born in Austria with Polish parents and had escaped the German invasion of Poland via Rumania, France and Malta. After arriving in England he joined No. 308 Squadron and then served as a flight commander with No. 303 Squadron before he returned to No. 308 Squadron as its commanding officer in March 1944. By the time Retinger arrived at Chailey he was already an

Armourers preparing Spitfires of No. 317 Squadron at Chailey in May 1944 during the period leading up to D-Day.

'ace' with at least five enemy aircraft confirmed as destroyed.

No. 317 Squadron was commanded by twenty-eight-year-old Squadron Leader Wlodzimiersz Miksa, another Polish veteran of the Battle of Britain. Miksa was born at Lodz in Poland and had joined the Polish Air Force in 1936. After the German invasion of Poland at the outbreak of the Second World War, Miksa fled his occupied homeland and arrived in England in July 1940 where he converted to the Hurricane and was posted to No. 303 Squadron at Leconfield. In January 1941 he helped form No. 315 Squadron at Acklington and he continued to serve with the squadron as a flight commander until April 1943. Miksa assumed command of No. 317 Squadron at Northolt in January 1944.

Having arrived at Chailey the squadrons immediately prepared for the forthcoming Allied invasion of Europe. All three squadrons were soon involved in *Ranger* and *Rhubarb* operations across the Channel, carrying out armed reconnaissance sorties and bombing attacks against military airfields and communications targets. The squadron pilots had already commenced bombing practice before arriving at Chailey and they were now able to put their training to good use. About half of the squadron's aircraft were capable of carrying out bombing sorties using either a single 500-lb bomb or 2 x 250-lb bombs. The first bombing sorties from Chailey were carried out by the Spitfires of No. 302 Squadron against a rail viaduct on 2 May.

On 12 May re-structuring within 2nd TAF saw the bigger fighter wings become Sectors and the Airfields, which had previously been numbered, became Wings using the corresponding number previously allocated. Chailey, which had been No. 131 Airfield, became No. 131 Wing and was tactically allocated to No. 18 Sector to operate alongside the Mustang IIIs of No. 133 Wing at Coolham and Spitfire IXs of No. 135 Wing at Selsey – all under the command and control of No. 84 Group.

Chailey was one of the RAF's most important ALGs. Not only was it the host airfield for No. 131 Wing but it was also HQ No. 18 Fighter Sector. Therefore, Chailey was commanded by Poland's

Spitfire IX and ground crew of the Polish No. 308 Squadron pictured at Chailey during the D-Day period.

highest ranking pilot, and the most highly decorated Pole serving with the RAF, Group Captain Alexander Gabszewicz. Born in Szawle, Kowno, in Poland in 1911, Gabszewicz joined the Polish Air Force in 1934. Like many of his Polish colleagues, he spent a short period fighting with the French before he fled to England and joined the RAF. He was posted to No. 607 Squadron during the latter weeks of the Battle of Britain. He commanded No. 316 Squadron in 1941 and later commanded No. 2 Polish Wing at Heston and then No. 1 Polish Wing at Northolt during 1943. He was then attached to the USAAF's 56th Fighter Group to fly P.47s. By the time he arrived at Chailey, Gabszewicz had been awarded the Polish *Virtuti Militari* 5th Class, the Polish Cross of Valour and two bars, the RAF's DFC and the French *Croix de Guerre*. He had also been credited with at least eight enemy aircraft destroyed plus many others shared or probables. Soon after arriving at Chailey came the announcement that his *Virtuti Militari* had been upgraded to 4th Class and of his award of the DSO. In addition to commanding No. 131 Wing at Chailey, command of No. 18 Fighter Sector gave Gabszewicz responsibility for two other wings: No. 133 Wing at Coolham and No. 135 Wing at Selsey – a total of nine squadrons were under his command.

On 21 May Nos 308 and 317 Squadrons were involved in an intense day of air operations against the German's transportation system in northern France. The day was a mix of success and failure for the 2nd TAF squadrons involved. Many trains were destroyed or hit but many Spitfires were lost during the day, including two belonging to No. 308 Squadron; both Spitfires were shot down by flak during an early morning raid to the west of Lillebonne with one of the pilots killed. The Spitfires were now flying with external fuel tanks to give the aircraft increased range. These tanks had originally been designed for fitting to Hurricanes but Spitfires had been modified to carry the tanks, which gave an additional forty-four gallons of fuel and allowed the pilots to reach as far as the German border as well as increasing the aircraft's endurance over the invasion area in the weeks to come.

During the D-Day operations all three squadrons were involved in flying low-level patrols over the beachheads and providing the invading ground forces with protection as they advanced from the beaches of Normandy. No fewer than four separate missions were flown by the three squadrons on D-Day itself with first take-offs

The farmhouse at Bower Farm was used by the officers at Chailey during the war.

soon after 5.00 a.m. and the last landings around 9.00 p.m. All three Polish squadron commanders were decorated for their gallantry and personal contribution to the successful air operations in support of the Allied invasion whilst operating from Chailey during the period April to June 1944. For leading No. 302 Squadron, Squadron Leader Marian Duryasz was awarded the DFC; Duryasz was later appointed to the Polish Staff at HQ 2nd TAF. Squadron Leader Witold Retinger was also awarded the DFC, as well as the Polish *Virtuti Militari* 5th Class, for leading No. 308 Squadron; Retinger remained in command of No. 308 Squadron until November when he was posted to HQ No. 11 Group as a liaison officer. Squadron Leader Wlodzimiersz Miksa was also awarded the DFC and Polish *Virtuti Militari* 5th Class for successfully leading No. 317 Squadron at Chailey; Miksa was also given a staff appointment, initially at HQ No. 12 Group and then at HQ Fighter Command.

With the beachhead secure the wing left Chailey on 28 June, which brought to an end Chailey's extremely short, but important, history as an airfield. The wing initially moved to Appledram and then to Ford (both in West Sussex) before moving across the Channel to Plumetot (B.10) on 3 August. Leading the wing on

Looking across Bower Farm and the site of the former airfield of Chailey.

operations across the Channel was Group Captain Alexander Gabszewicz.

Although extremely short-lived, the airfield at Chailey had served its purpose well and coped with the short period of intense air operations. There had been a few problems with operating Spitfires from the metal runway but by and large things had gone according to plan. With flying operations over, the Sommerfield track metal runway was pulled up for use elsewhere, although the airfield was retained until the end of the war. After the war the site reverted to agricultural use. Chailey airshows were held as recently as 2000 and 2004, serving as a dedication to the Polish pilots and ground personnel who served at Chailey during 1944.

Today the site is Bower Farm, which is in Beresford Lane. A memorial to these brave men now stands adjacent to the new Plough Inn; the original pub having been demolished to facilitate taking off and landing. If approaching Chailey from the north, take the A272 from Haywards Heath eastwards to Chailey Crossroads. Turn right on the A275 south towards South Chailey. Turn right into Mill Lane, which then becomes Honeypot Lane. At the end of Honeypot Lane turn right at the T-junction into South Road. It is worth stopping at the Plough Inn on the left to admire the splendid

The memorial at Chailey stands outside the Plough Inn and provides a wonderful setting for light refreshment if in the local area.

memorial to those who served at Chailey. After the memorial turn right into Beresford Lane. After about a mile Bower Farm can be seen on the right and the road then becomes Plumpton Road. The site of the former airfield is on the right and left of the road. If approaching from the south, directions are from Lewes. From the A27 at Lewes take the A275 north to South Chailey. Then turn left into Mill Lane and follow the directions above.

Squadron	Dates at Chailey	Aircraft Type
302 'Poznanski' Squadron	26 Apr – 28 Jun 1944	Spitfire IX
308 'Krakowski' Sqn	26 Apr – 28 Jun 1944	Spitfire IX
317 'Wilenski' Squadron	26 Apr – 28 Jun 1944	Spitfire IX

Coolham

On D-Day Coolham was an Advanced Landing Ground of 2nd TAF and home to three Mustang squadrons of No. 133 Wing, No. 84 Group. Coolham's short aviation history lasted no more than three years and the land reverted to agriculture after the Second World War.

Situated 6 miles to the south-west of Horsham in West Sussex, Coolham is another of the least known of the airfields used by 2nd TAF during the D-Day air operations. Like Chailey in East Sussex, the airfield of Coolham has a very short history. It was constructed in 1942, solely for the use during the period of the D-Day operations, and the site reverted to agricultural use after the Second World War.

Coolham was an ALG rather than an airfield. The site was at first identified in the late spring of 1942. The terrain was generally flat and the close proximity to the amenities in the towns of Billingshurst and Horsham made it an attractive option. The area chosen for construction was the agricultural land and woodland to the south of Coolham village on the eastern side of the B2139 road, which runs towards the village of Thakenham. Initial work began in early 1943 but it was not until the summer that the major work was done when personnel from the Airfield Construction Squadrons moved in. Two Sommerfield track runways were laid, which were essentially runways of heavy steel netting held rigid by steel bars secured by pickets, the idea being that aircraft operations would only generally be conducted during fair weather and not during the winter. The main runway was 1,500 yards long and orientated in a south-east to north-west direction. The second runway, just over 1,200 yards, was orientated south-west/north-east. Thirty-six hardened aircraft dispersals were also constructed and four blister hangars erected. The air traffic control tower was a mobile caravan and tents and marquees were used for all other purposes. Work was completed by the end of March 1944.

Coolham was designated No. 133 Airfield, within the organisation of No. 84 Group, and was under the command of Group Captain Tadeusz Nowierski as the airfield had been allocated two Polish fighter squadrons. The two squadrons both arrived at Coolham on 1 April, although each squadron's ground

crew had already made the journey south to ensure that domestic
and technical tented facilities were already in place by the time the
squadron arrived.

No. 306 Squadron was commanded by Squadron Leader
Stanislaw Lapka. Born in Warsaw in 1915, Lapka had served with
No. 302 Squadron during the Battle of Britain and he took
command of No. 306 Squadron at Llanbedr in January 1944. The
squadron then spent the next few days transiting aircraft in and out
of Coolham as this was also the period that No. 306 Squadron was
in the process of converting from Spitfire VBs to the Mustang III.
The second squadron was No. 315 'Deblinksi' Squadron. This
squadron had formed at Acklington in January 1941 and, like No.
306 Squadron, had been based at various stations during its
existence. The squadron had flown from its base at Llanbedr in
Wales to Heston three days before making the final transit to
Coolham. No. 315 Squadron was under the command of the
legendary Polish ace, Squadron Leader Eugeniusz Horbaczewski.
Born in Kiev, Russia in 1917, Horbaczewski had joined the Polish
Air Force in 1937. After the German invasion of Poland he escaped
through Rumania to France and then on to England. Horbaczewski
then joined the RAF and later distinguished himself during the
North African campaign whilst serving with the Desert Air Force;
during March to April 1943 he claimed five victories in less than
four weeks. Returning to the UK, Horbaczewski took command of
No. 315 Squadron in February 1944. By then he had been credited
with at least eleven confirmed kills and had been awarded the DSO.
During the first few weeks at Coolham both Polish squadrons
completed their conversion to the Mustang. They were joined by
No. 129 Squadron, which arrived at Coolham on 3 April under the
command of twenty-three-year-old Squadron Leader 'Wag' Haw.
Having distinguished himself whilst serving with No. 151 Wing in
Murmansk, Russia, during January 1941, Haw was one of only four
RAF recipients of the Russian Order of Lenin.

The first operational sorties were flown from Coolham at the end
of April. On 26 April, No. 129 Squadron and No. 315 Squadron flew
a fighter sweep over Beauvais; unfortunately, No. 129 Squadron lost
an aircraft shot down by flak. No. 306 Squadron flew its first
operational sorties just three days later. On 12 May restructuring
within 2nd TAF saw the bigger fighter wings become Sectors and
the Airfields, which had previously been numbered, became Wings

Stanislaw Skalski led No. 133 Wing at Coolham during the period of the D-Day operations. He was the highest scoring Polish pilot during the German's invasion of September 1939 and was eventually credited with twenty-four enemy aircraft destroyed.

using the corresponding number previously allocated. Coolham, which had been No. 133 Airfield, became No. 133 Wing and was tactically allocated to No. 18 Sector to operate alongside the Spitfire IXs of No. 131 Wing at Chailey and No. 135 Wing at Selsey – all under the command and control of No. 84 Group.

The Coolham Wing was commanded by another legendary Polish ace, Wing Commander Stanislaw Skalski. Born in Russia in 1915, Stanislaw Skalski joined the Polish Air Force in 1936. Like many of his colleagues, he escaped to England following the German invasion of Poland at the start of the Second World War. By then he had already become an ace with six confirmed kills during the first four days of September 1939. Having joined the RAF in August 1940, he soon added to his tally whilst serving with No. 501 Squadron and by the end of the Battle of Britain he had brought his personal total to thirteen kills, although he had a lucky escape on 5 September when he was shot down and badly burned. Skalski returned to operations and was posted as a flight commander to No. 306 Squadron. Whilst serving with No. 306 Squadron he added five further kills to his total during 1941 after which he was posted initially to No. 316 Squadron and then to command No. 317

Squadron. During 1943 Skalski served with the Polish Fighting Team of volunteers who went to North Africa to operate with the Desert Air Force. By the time he returned to the UK in October 1943 to take up his new command as Officer Commanding No. 131 Wing at Northolt, Skalski had been credited with at least eighteen kills and had been awarded the DFC and two bars, the Polish *Virtuti Militari* and the Polish Cross of Valour with three bars. In April 1944, at the age of twenty-nine, he was given command of No. 133 Wing at Coolham.

During a *Ramrod* mission in the late afternoon of 18 May, the wing scored its first victory when Mustangs of No. 306 Squadron shot down a Heinkel He111 to the north-east of Nevers in France. Amongst the Polish pilots to share in the destruction of the Heinkel was twenty-four-year-old Flight Lieutenant Wladyslaw Potocki from Cracow. This was the first of his successes whilst serving with the squadron and he would go on to be credited with four kills during his time at Coolham. During the evening of 25 May No. 315 Squadron was taking part in a *Ranger* across France when the pilots spotted two Arado AR96 trainers over Bourges; the trainers were no match for the Mustangs and both trainers were soon shot down as the squadron pilots added to their total.

The wing not only flew operations but also trained with the Army in preparation for the forthcoming Allied invasion of Europe. There was also much to do for the ground crew as the squadron's re-equipment with the Mustang had to be completed as soon as possible. The Mustang proved to be a very capable and versatile aircraft. It could carry two 500-lb bombs for short-range bombing attacks over northern France or two external fuel tanks for longer-range escort missions over Germany; these would often be in excess of five hours. The range and endurance of the Mustang made it an excellent aircraft for long-range escort sorties. An example of how the Coolham squadrons were used in this role is evident from the efforts of No. 315 Squadron during May when the squadron flew more than 300 sorties, most of which were long-range escort.

During the first few days of June the weather was not good. There was no flying from Coolham on the 4th and little flying on the 5th. However, it was obvious to those at Coolham that something was building up as there was much movement of heavy transport in the local area. During the evening of 5 June the pilots were briefed that the invasion was due to start in the early hours of the following day. Everyone was up early the following morning and they listened to speeches about the invasion as the events of the historic day unfolded.

For the D-Day operations on 6 June No. 133 Wing was allocated the responsibility of providing fighter escort for the second wave of gliders and tugs. Having listened to all the early morning excitement on the radio during the morning, the wing pilots found the rest of the day frustrating and a disappointment as most of the day was spent sitting around. Eventually, the pilots were called for briefing around 5.00 p.m. and the wing got airborne in the early evening to escort bombers across the Channel to attack targets on the eastern flank of the invasion area. Wing Commander Skalski led the thirty-six Mustangs involved and, although the Coolham pilots saw many friendly aircraft around, there was little in the way of enemy air activity at that time; one enemy Focke-Wulf FW190 was shot down to the south-west of Caen by Flight Lieutenant Allan Hancock and Warrant Officer William Rigby of No. 129 Squadron.

If D-Day itself had largely proved to be uneventful for the Coolham Wing, the following day was quite the opposite and proved to be Coolham's most hectic and momentous day. The wing was airborne at first light, armed with 500-lb bombs, for an armed reconnaissance mission over the area of Argentan. Although the weather was once again poor with a cloud base of less than 2,000 feet in the target area, the Mustangs carried out a successful attack against the railway station at Argentan. Having returned to Coolham, the wing was airborne again just two hours later; this time for a bombing attack against the railway marshalling yards at Dreux. More bombing sorties were flown by the wing during the afternoon, in particular a concentrated attack against the railway and road junctions around Sees, and again in the evening; the main attack being against the railway at Ecoucher. It was more of the same on the 8th and the weather was too poor to fly on the 9th. Bombing operations over the invasion area recommenced on 10 June but there was little flying, again due to poor weather, the following day.

This period for the Coolham Wing was a mixture of sitting around waiting for suitable weather over the invasion area, followed by maximum effort with little rest for the pilots between sorties. The operational tempo remained the same for the following week and then the squadrons prepared to move out of Coolham as

Mustangs of No 129 Squadron at Coolham painted with the now-familiar black and white invasion stripes.

the Allied advance into Normandy gathered momentum. On 22 June Nos 129 and 306 Squadrons left Coolham, initially for Holmsley South and then on to Brenzett in Kent; No. 315 Squadron followed on 26 June. The three squadrons had been at Coolham for less than three months. During that time the Wing had flown forty-one specific *Ramrod* missions, numerous armed reconnaissance *Rangers* and *Rodeos* over northern France and had destroyed twenty-eight enemy aircraft. Unfortunately, there had inevitably been losses. During May and June 1944 the wing lost twenty-one Mustangs with the loss of thirteen pilots; two of those pilots were Allan Hancock and William Rigby of No. 129 Squadron who had shared in the success of D-Day when they had shot down a FW190 near Caen.

On 30 June No. 135 Wing was briefly transferred to Coolham from Selsey. The Wing flew Spitfire IXs and consisted of No. 222 Squadron, under the command of Squadron Leader David Cox, No. 349 (Belgian) Squadron, commanded by Squadron Leader the Count Yvan du Monceau de Bergendael, and No. 485 Squadron RNZAF under the command of Squadron Leader John Niven. On 1 July the Wing flew as fighter escort for a bombing raid on V-1 sites in the Pas de Calais. The Wing then flew Ranger sorties over the Normandy area on the 2nd and 3rd. The Wing's short stay at Coolham was soon over when it transferred to Funtington on 4 July.

Coolham's short-lived history as an ALG was over as no other squadrons operated from the site after No. 135 Wing left. The last recorded flight at Coolham was in January 1945 when an American B-24 Liberator made an emergency landing at Coolham; the aircraft was soon repaired and flew back to its base a few days later. At the end of the Second World War, work started to return the site back to agriculture and was complete a year later.

Stanislaw Skalski survived the war and went on to become a general in the Polish Air Force but not before he had first been imprisoned by the Russians between 1948 and 1956 for his connections with the West; one year of which had been under the threat of the death sentence for espionage. During his latter years, Stanislaw Skalski returned to the UK a number of times; one such visit was to Coolham in 1994 for the unveiling of a memorial to No. 133 Wing. Stanislaw Skalski died in Warsaw in 2004, aged eighty-nine. 'Wag' Haw, who commanded No. 129 Squadron at Coolham, also survived the war and left the RAF in 1951. He later ran a pub at Adversane, near Coolham, and then worked in the pet food

The memorial at Coolham can be found in the centre of the village at the crossroads in front of the Selsey Arms pub.

business. He died in 1993. Stanislaw Lapka, commander of No. 306 Squadron, survived the war and settled in England; he died in 1978. Eugeniusz Horbaczewski, commander of No. 315 Squadron, was not so lucky; he was killed soon after leaving Coolham. Outnumbered by FW190s over the Beauvais area on 18 August 1944, Horbaczewski was shot down and killed but not before he personally destroyed three of the FW190s.

In 1994 a memorial was unveiled at Coolham to commemorate the vital role played by the squadrons and personnel who served at the airfield during 1944. It can be found at the Coolham crossroads in the front garden of the Selsey Arms pub. All the land was fully converted back to agriculture and the only reminders are some farm tracks marking where the airfield perimeter track once was. The village of Coolham can be reached by taking the A272 south-east from Billingshurst or west from the A24 London to Worthing road. The memorial can be found in the centre of the village and the site of the former airfield is immediately to the south-east of the village, on the eastern side of the B2139 Thakeham Road.

Squadron	Dates at Coolham	Aircraft Type
306 'Torunski' Squadron	1 Apr – 22 Jun 1944	Mustang III
315 'Deblinski' Squadron	1 Apr – 26 Jun 1944	Mustang III
129 Squadron	6 Apr – 22 Jun 1944	Mustang III
222 Squadron	30 Jun – 4 Jul 1944	Spitfire IX
349 (Belgian) Squadron	30 Jun – 4 Jul 1944	Spitfire IX
485 Squadron RNZAF	30 Jun – 4 Jul 1944	Spitfirc IX

Deanland

Yet another relatively unknown Advanced Landing Ground in Sussex, Deanland was home to three squadrons of Spitfires on D-Day under the command and control of No. 11 Group ADGB. After the war the land reverted to agriculture but the airfield has since been reactivated and is now considered to be the home of light aviation in East Sussex.

The airfield of Deanland is situated about 4 miles to the north-west of Hailsham in East Sussex. Like Chailey and Coolham, previously covered, Deanland was an ALG rather than an airfield, and was used briefly during the period either side of D-Day.

Land near the village of Ripe was surveyed and requisitioned in early 1943. Consistent with the design of other ALGs, two Sommerfield track runways were laid and four blister hangars erected. There was no permanent construction, although concrete

The oak tree at Deanland was planted in memory of the pilots who died whilst operating from the airfield during the war.

hard standings were laid. Work was completed by the end of March 1944 ready for three Polish squadrons to move in to Deanland; the three squadrons were No. 302 'Poznanski' Squadron, No. 308 'Krakowski' Squadron and No. 317 'Wilenski' Squadron, which all arrived from Northolt on 1 April. The squadrons were all equipped with Spitfire IXs and had recently converted to the fighter-bomber role but their stay at Deanland was short-lived and all three squadrons moved to nearby Chailey on 26 April. However, within three days of the Polish squadrons departing, Deanland once again had three more squadrons in residence. Two squadrons arrived from Coltishall, which were No. 64 Squadron, commanded by twenty-nine-year-old Squadron Leader John Mackenzie from New Zealand, and No. 611 Squadron, commanded by twenty-two-year-old Squadron Leader William Douglas. The third squadron was No. 234 Squadron, commanded by Squadron Leader Peter Arnott, which arrived from Bolt Head.

Deanland was designated No. 149 Wing on 15 May. At that time, Deanland was still under the command of HQ 11 Group ADGB. All three squadrons were operating the Spitfire V and the squadrons spent their early days providing fighter escort for light-bombers from No. 2 Group and American bombers from the Ninth Air Force, which were continually attacking the German defences along the North Atlantic and Channel coasts. Although the Spitfire V was old in comparison with the Spitfire IX and Mustangs also in service with 2nd TAF, its performance at low-level was good and it was ideal for carrying out air-to-ground attacks against trains, vehicles or even shipping when required.

On D-Day, 6 June, No. 611 Squadron was airborne at 3.00 a.m., before first light, and won the respectable distinction of being the first British fighter squadron over the beachhead on D-Day, operating mainly over the western part of the invasion area above the American V Corps beach of *Omaha* and the British XXX Corps beach *Gold*. No. 234 Squadron was also heavily involved in the air activity on D-Day. Its task was to provide fighter escort for the tugs and gliders, and the pilots were then given freedom to attack German defensive positions. When the weather allowed, the Deanland Wing continued to fly patrols over the beachhead during the next few days but no enemy aircraft were encountered until the evening of 10 June when Squadron Leader William Douglas, the Commanding Officer of No. 611 Squadron, shot down a Junkers

Ju88 to the south-west of Saintenay. It was his fifth kill of the war.

As Deanland was located on the V-1 rocket path towards London, there was little rest for the personnel as the anti-aircraft defences were almost continually in action day and night. No. 149 Wing moved out of Deanland during the period 19–23 June and the squadrons went west to Harrowbeer in Devon and Predannack in Cornwall for re-equipping and a well-earned rest. There then followed a short period of four weeks when there were no squadrons based at Deanland. By the time the Spitfires of No. 91 Squadron and No. 322 (Dutch) Squadron moved into Deanland from West Malling on 21 July, command and control of Deanland had been passed to No. 85 Group within 2nd TAF.

No. 91 Squadron was commanded by Squadron Leader Norman Kynaston. Originally posted to the squadron as a flight commander in November 1942, Kynaston had assumed command of the squadron in August 1943. The following month he shot down three Focke-Wulf FW190s over France and shared in the destruction of two more. He scored his fourth kill in October, another FW190 over France, and was awarded the DFC. Norman Kynaston also became a V-1 ace during the summer of 1944, personally accounting for seventeen V-1 flying bombs heading for London. Sadly, however, his days were soon over. Whilst leading a squadron sweep over Belgium on 15 August, his Spitfire was hit by flak. Although he was seen to bale out of his aircraft over the French coast, Norman Kynaston's body was never found. Soon after came the announcement of a bar to his DFC. Norman Kynaston DFC and bar was twenty-nine years old and he is commemorated on the Runnymede Memorial.

Another loss suffered by No. 91 Squadron during this period was Captain Jean-Marie Maridor. Born in France in 1920, Maridor had trained as a pilot in the *Armée de l'Air*. Fleeing occupied France in a fishing boat, Maridor joined the RAF as a sergeant pilot. He joined No. 91 Squadron in February 1941 by which time he had been commissioned. Apart from a short rest period as an instructor, Maridor spent the rest of his operational flying with the squadron. By the time he arrived at Deanland, Jean-Marie Maridor had been credited with at least three kills, plus a share in several others. He had been awarded the DFC and bar and a French *Croix de Guerre*. Maridor had also been credited with the destruction of ten V-1 flying bombs, and it was whilst destroying his eleventh that his own life was to end in tragedy. Having taken off from Deanland on 3 August, Jean-Marie Maridor was chasing a V-1. Having hit the V-1 once, he could see it was falling in the vicinity of a hospital. He continued to close on the V-1, determined to destroy it before it hit the ground. He succeeded but tragically his aircraft came down in the explosion. His aircraft crashed in a field near Beneden, Kent. Jean-Marie Maridor DFC and bar was just twenty-three years old.

When No. 322 (Dutch) Squadron arrived at Deanland it was still a relatively new squadron, having formed in June 1943 from a cadre of Dutch pilots serving with No. 167 Squadron at the time. Equipped with the powerful and high-performance Griffon-engined Spitfire XIV, the squadron was considered well equipped to take on the increasing number of V-1 flying bombs that crossed southern England *en route* for London. This certainly proved to be the case and the squadron accounted for over 100 flying bombs during the summer of 1944, many of which were shot down whilst operating from Deanland.

Deanland became home to a third squadron on 16 August 1944 when No. 345 (Free French) Squadron moved in from nearby

The plaque beneath the oak tree.

Shoreham. The squadron soon re-equipped with the Spitfire IX and adopted French roundels and fin flashes. As the intensity of the V-1 attacks against London decreased, the three squadrons prepared to move across the Channel. The squadrons left Deanland one by one during the second week of October, initially for Biggin Hill before the Dutch and Free French squadrons were then moved on across to mainland Europe. No. 91 Squadron, however, remained in England and moved to Manston where it remained until the end of the war.

Within weeks of the last Spitfires moving out, Deanland closed. The Sommerfield track was eventually lifted and slowly the evidence that the site had been an active wartime airfield began to disappear as the land reverted to agricultural use once more. Ownership of the land was passed on and eventually belonged to a farmer, Richard Chandless, who had an interest in aircraft and he reactivated the site as an airfield in 1963. Mr Chandless initially operated his own aircraft from a field and he then started selling new and used aircraft from Deanland as well as allowing other aircraft owners to operate from the site. By then, Mr Chandless had laid out a runway of some 500 yards in length about half a mile

The airfield at Deanland has been reactivated and is now considered to be the home for light aviation in East Sussex.

south of Deanland Wood Park. He then constructed a small hangar and Deanland became increasingly more active, one of the main reasons being that there were no other small airfields in the immediate area.

In the early 1990s the land was sold on again to the present owners, Gerry Price, David Brook and Roy Brook and has since been operated by Deanland Airfield LLP. On 6 June 1994, the fiftieth anniversary of D-Day, a special day was held at Deanland and a plaque showing the insignia of the Deanland squadrons was donated to the Ripe Parish Church. The plaque was presented by Air Chief Marshal Sir Neil Wheeler who had been present with Winston Churchill on D-Day itself. An oak tree was planted in remembrance of those pilots who died whilst operating from the airfield during the war.

Most reminders of the war have long disappeared but the fact that Deanland has been reactivated is a marvellous tribute to this former wartime airfield; today Deanland is proud to be considered as the premier home for light aviation in East Sussex. It can be found by taking the A22 north-westwards from Hailsham. After 3 miles, and just before the B2124 towards Lewes, take the minor road south-westwards towards the village of Ripe; this is Deanland Road. After just over a mile the road takes a sharp right and then a sharp left; the road then becomes Ripe Lane. The airfield is on the right about a mile short of the village of Ripe.

Squadron	Dates at Deanland	Aircraft Type
302 'Poznanski' Squadron	1 – 26 Apr 1944	Spitfire IX
308 'Krakowski' Squadron	1 – 26 Apr 1944	Spitfire IX
317 'Wilenski' Squadron	1 – 26 Apr 1944	Spitfire IX
234 Squadron	29 Apr – 19 Jun 1944	Spitfire V
64 Squadron	29 Apr – 23 Jun 1944	Spitfire V
611 Squadron	29 Apr – 23 Jun 1944	Spitfire V & Spitfire IX
91 Squadron	21 Jul – 7 Oct 1944	Spitfire XIV & Spitfire IX
322 (Dutch) Squadron	21 Jul – 10 Oct 1944	Spitfire XIV & Spitfire IX
345 (Free French) Squadron	16 Aug – 18 Oct 1944	Spitfire V & Spitfire IX

Friston

Now centred on Gayles Farm and overlooking the Seven Sisters Country Park, Friston's forward location on the South Downs made it an ideal site for an Advanced Landing Ground during the Second World War. On D-Day Friston was home to two Spitfire squadrons of No. 11 Group ADGB.

Just 4 miles to the west of Eastbourne in East Sussex is the former airfield of Friston. Its origins date back to just before the Second World War when it was a private landing ground and was known as Gayles or sometimes East Dean. During the early part of the Second World War, Friston's forward location on the South Downs made it an ideal location for use as an emergency landing ground for squadrons of Fighter Command.

At that time Friston was an all-grass airfield with basic facilities. During 1941 and early 1942 the airfield's facilities were upgraded and command and control of the airfield was given to Kenley. In

Looking west across the former airfield of Friston towards Seaford and the Channel. It really is a most wonderful location and was the setting for the popular TV series Piece of Cake during the late 1980s.

June 1942 the first Hurricanes of Nos 32 and 253 Squadrons moved in, from West Malling and Hibaldstow respectively, to become the first resident squadrons at Friston. The two squadrons briefly operated together as a wing but both squadrons moved out after a month. However, although there were no permanent squadrons based at Friston, the airfield was used as a forward operating base by detachments of fighters from Kenley. Indeed, both Nos 32 and 253 Squadrons operated out of Friston during the Dieppe Raid on 19 August 1942.

An increasing number of raids against targets along the south coast of England led to Spitfire XIIs of No. 41 Squadron briefly moving into Friston from Biggin Hill during May and June 1943. Improvements to the airfield meant that Friston could be used during the winter of 1943–4 and No. 349 (Belgian) Squadron moved in on 22 October 1943 having moved south from Acklington. The Belgian squadron remained at Friston until March 1944, spending most of its time flying fighter sweeps across the Channel; by this time, command and control of Friston had been passed to Biggin Hill.

On 11 March 1944 No. 41 Squadron returned to Friston to replace the Belgian squadron. The squadron flew mainly *Ramrod* and *Rhubarb* missions from Friston until the end of April when it moved to Bolt Head. During the final build up to the Allied invasion of Europe, Friston was home to two Spitfire V squadrons: No. 501 Squadron and No. 350 (Belgian) Squadron. Command and control had once again been passed on, this time to Tangmere as part of No. 11 Group ADGB. The two squadrons operated as a wing under the command of Wing Commander Don Kingaby who was officially a staff officer at HQ Fighter Command at the time although he did manage to attach himself to No. 501 Squadron to fly operationally during this period. By that time of the war Don Kingaby had been personally credited with twenty-one kills plus many more either shared or officially counted as 'probables'. He was the only ever recipient of the DFM and two bars, and had also been awarded the DSO in March 1943.

On D-Day itself the Friston Wing was airborne early and the pilots soon found themselves over the Normandy beaches, although there were no engagements with the enemy. The Friston Wing continued to operate over Normandy as the Alllies made their breakout from the beachhead. Don Kingaby scored his last success of the war on 30 June whilst again flying with No. 501 Squadron; he shared in the destruction of a Messerschmitt Bf109 over the Cazelle area.

At the beginning of July No. 501 and No. 350 (Belgian) Squadrons left Friston for Westhampnett. The two squadrons were replaced at Friston by Nos 41 and 610 Squadrons, which were equipped with more powerful Spitfires to combat the increasing number of V-1 flying bombs targeted against London. No. 41 Squadron did not stay at Friston long and left for Lympne just nine days later. It was replaced by the Polish No. 316 'Warszawski' Squadron, equipped with Mustangs. The two squadrons enjoyed success during the anti-Diver patrols and their tally soon mounted. By September, however, the V-1 threat had reduced and both Friston squadrons moved out and the airfield once again reverted to being an Emergency Landing Ground.

This building was believed to be used as a medical block at Friston and has remained until the present day.

After the Second World War, Friston was placed on care and maintenance. The airfield was used for gliding purposes until the 1950s. In 1988 film crews arrived at Friston to film the six-part TV production *Piece of Cake*, which was based on the novel by Derek Robinson and depicted the life of a RAF fighter squadron during the early days of the Second World War.

The site can be found midway along the A259 between Eastbourne and Seaford. When travelling from the Seaford direction, the site of the former airfield can be found about one mile before the village of Friston on the right hand side of the road. On the left side of the road is woodland. Parking is difficult as the road is narrow and often busy, and there are few places to pull in. Very little evidence of the former airfield has survived; the area is centred on Gayles Farm, which now forms a quiet backdrop to the Seven Sisters Country Park. To the north is Friston Forest, to the east is East Dean and to the west is the country park. Just half a mile to the

Gayles Farm was used by the officers at Friston during the Second World War and is now the home of my host Derry Robinson.

south is the South Downs Way and the famous white cliffs looking towards Beachy Head to the east and out over the Channel.

Gayles Farm is privately owned by Derry and Roz Robinson and there is no public access to the former airfield, although the Stables can be hired for short self-catering breaks; the Stables afford privacy as well as easy access to the countryside. The address is: Stables, Gayles, Friston, Nr Eastbourne, East Sussex, BN20 0BA. The telephone number is 07721 023 845. I thoroughly recommend a stay in one of the most beautiful locations along the south-east coast, with the most wonderful hospitality.

Squadron	Dates at Friston	Aircraft Type
349 (Belgian) Squadron	22 Oct 43 – 11 Mar 44	Spitfire V
41 Squadron	11 Mar – 29 Apr 44	Spitfire XII
501 Squadron	30 Apr – 2 Jul 44	Spitfire V
350 (Belgian) Squadron	25 Apr – 4 Jul 44	Spitfire V
41 Squadron	2 – 11 Jul 44	Spitfire XII
610 Squadron	2 Jul – 12 Sep 44	Spitfire XIV
316 'Warszawski' Squadron	11 Jul – 27 Aug 44	Mustang III

Gatwick

First used in the 1930s, Gatwick is now London's second major international airport but on D-Day it was a 2nd TAF airfield and home to Mustangs and Spitfires of No. 35 (Recce) Wing, No. 84 Group.

Although rarely remembered for its role in wartime, the airfield of Gatwick needs little or no introduction. Many of us have passed through this vast international airport *en route* to holiday or business destinations but seldom do we give thought to the many airmen and airwomen who served at Gatwick during the Second World War. The airfield played a part during the Battle of Britain and was particularly busy during the build up to the Allied invasion of Europe and the period immediately after. Only when the Allies started to gain a strong foothold in Europe, did the squadrons start to leave.

Situated to the north of Crawley in West Sussex, Gatwick was first used as an airfield in 1930. By 1936 it had developed as an airport but was often used by the RAF during the latter years building up to the Second World War. During the Battle of Britain Gatwick was used by No. 11 Group as an emergency satellite for Kenley and by the Defiants of No. 141 Squadron, in the role of night-fighters. The airfield was also used by Lysanders of No. 26 Squadron, in support of Army Cooperation Command.

The link with the Army took another step forward when control of Gatwick was transferred from Fighter Command to Army Cooperation Command in January 1941, and No. 26 Squadron was joined by No. 239 Squadron in support of Army exercises. Both squadrons remained at Gatwick until early 1942 by which time improvements had been made to the airfield, particularly regarding the runways.

Gatwick played a major part in the famous Dieppe Raid on 19 August 1942, code-named Operation *Jubilee*. The raid was carried out by Canadian troops supported by British Commandos and American Rangers with the objectives of destroying local defences and airfields near the town, and capturing or destroying any German invasion barges or vessels in the harbour. The air support given to the operation involved the largest number of aircraft ever assembled and included more than sixty fighter squadrons of the

RAF. Four of these squadrons were Mustang squadrons based at Gatwick, which happened to be the only Mustangs involved on the day. The two resident squadrons at Gatwick, Nos 26 and 239, were joined by two Canadian squadrons, Nos 400 and 414 RCAF Squadrons. The RAF flew nearly 3,000 sorties on the day, which included fifty sorties flown by the Mustangs; RAF losses included ten Mustangs from Gatwick. The squadron that suffered the worst was No. 26 Squadron, which lost five Mustangs destroyed and another damaged; three pilots were killed and two taken as prisoners of war. No. 239 Squadron lost three Mustangs and had another damaged; two pilots were killed and one taken prisoner. The two Canadian squadrons each lost a Mustang with one pilot killed and another wounded. It was a dark day for Gatwick – six pilots were killed, one wounded and three taken as prisoners of war. However, despite the losses, the RAF claimed a great victory on the day, although the Canadian troops on the ground suffered considerable losses.

There were changes of personnel at Gatwick during the winter and early months of 1943. In July 1943 Gatwick became No. 129 Airfield, with Mustangs of No. 414 Squadron RCAF in residence, but the squadron soon moved out and the airfield was placed on care and maintenance in August 1943. In October two Spitfire IX squadrons, Nos 19 and 65, arrived at Gatwick but they only stayed for just over a week. They were replaced by Canadian Mustangs of No. 430 Squadron RCAF, which remained at Gatwick until the beginning of April 1944, and No. 414 Squadron RCAF, which returned once more and this time remained until February 1944. As part of No. 83 Group, 2nd TAF, the two squadrons took part in various sorties across the Channel, including tactical reconnaissance of enemy radar and communications establishments, fuel dumps and anything else of tactical importance to the Allies as preparations were taking place for the Allied invasion of Europe. The squadrons also took part in offensive sweeps across the Channel looking for any enemy aircraft attempting to attack ports and towns in southern England.

Improvements to the airfield took place during the winter period. By now the primary role of No. 414 Squadron during early 1944 was photographic reconnaissance, although the squadron did fly the occasional *Rhubarb* and *Ranger* sorties across the Channel. The squadron pilots enjoyed the occasional air-to-air success. For

A Mosquito of No. 4 Squadron, part of No. 35 (Recce) Wing, at Gatwick in April 1944.

example, on 28 January four Mustangs were over the Chartres area when the Canadians came across two AR96 trainers. Two of the squadron's pilots shared one of the trainers, which came down to the east of Chartres. The formation was then attacked by two Messerschmitt Bf109s in the local area; both Bf109s were shot down. One of the successful pilots that day was Flight Lieutenant Gordon Wonnacott from Edmonton, Alberta. The Bf109 he destroyed came down to the north-east of Chartres; it was his first kill of the war, although he had shared in the destruction of a Focke-Wulf FW190 two months earlier. On 5 February No. 414 Squadron RCAF left Gatwick and was replaced the following month by No. 168 Squadron.

On 1 April the designation No. 129 Airfield moved from Gatwick to Odiham to become part of No. 15 Wing, leaving the way clear for three different squadrons to make their home at Gatwick. It would be these three squadrons that would operate from Gatwick as No. 35 (Recce) Wing, under the command of No. 84 Group, during the D-Day period. The first two of these squadrons arrived on 4 April from Sawbridgeworth. No. 2 Squadron was equipped with Mustang IIs and No. 4 Squadron was equipped with Spitfire XIs and a few Mosquito XVIs. Both of these squadrons were used in a variety of roles, including Army cooperation, as well as more recently carrying out tactical reconnaissance missions over France and the Low Countries. The third squadron to make up the wing was No. 268 Squadron, equipped with Mustangs, which flew in from Dundonald on 8 April.

The wing was led by twenty-nine-year-old Group Captain Peter Donkin DSO. Born in New Zealand, Peter Donkin had joined the RAF as a cadet at Cranwell in 1933. He was a commanding officer who liked to lead from the front. On 13 April he flew a tactical reconnaissance sortie over the Belgian coast in one of the wing's Mustangs. Whilst over the coast he was hit by flak and had to bale out. Fortunately, after an extensive search over the next few days, Donkin was found safe in his dinghy; he had spent six days in the water.

During the middle of May No. 4 Squadron started to convert one of its flights from Mosquitos to Spitfire XIs and within a few weeks the squadron had completed its conversion to its new type. On 23 May No. 2 Squadron lost one of its Mustangs on a reconnaissance sortie when it was hit by flak to the south-west of Etretat. The pilot, Flight Lieutenant Furneaux, managed to bale out over the sea and was fortunately picked up by a friendly air-sea rescue unit.

During the afternoon of the following day, two Mustangs of No. 268 Squadron took part in a low-level reconnaissance mission over a German radar station at Neufchatel. D-Day was now just a matter of days away and 2nd TAF was taking deliberate action to destroy the German's radar chain along the northern coast of France. There were too many sites to attack and destroy all of them but if the Allies could neutralise as many as possible then it would enable them to gain the element of surprise during the crucial early hours of D-Day. Reconnaissance of these sites and the subsequent results of the attacks by the 2nd TAF squadrons were given high priority.

The reconnaissance pilots involved in these missions did all that was necessary to get the pictures back to base. One example was Flight Lieutenant Winslow, one of the two Gatwick reconnaissance pilots that day. His Mustang was hit by flak whilst flying extremely low over the radar station. His cockpit filled with smoke and so he jettisoned the canopy and flew back across the Channel. Having decided to make an emergency landing at Brenzett in Kent, Winslow could not lower his undercarriage and so he had to make a crash-landing on the airfield. Despite his injuries Winslow had managed to complete his mission, although his Mustang was written-off. Later that afternoon another squadron pilot, Flying Officer Ashford, was also hit by flak to the south-east of Boulogne. Ashford was badly wounded but managed to complete his photo run before returning to base when he was rushed to hospital. These were typical examples of the bravery of the reconnaissance pilots of No. 35 (Recce) Wing during this crucial period immediately prior to the D-Day landings.

All three Gatwick squadrons were involved during the D-Day operations of 6 June. The two Mustang squadrons were involved in aerial spotting for the Royal Navy's bombardment of coastal targets and the task of No. 4 Squadron was to provide tactical photographic reconnaissance over Normandy. This proved particularly hazardous for the Mustang pilots due to a mix of poor weather and

North Terminal is a familiar sight to business travellers and holidaymakers but there is no evidence of Gatwick's former wartime days.

heavy ground defences. The first casualty was a Mustang of No. 268 Squadron during the early hours of the invasion; the pilot was killed. Cloud over the landing beaches and Normandy also prevented the Spitfire pilots from achieving their task on D-Day and continuing poor weather over the invasion area meant that it would be several days before the Spitfires could offer any significant contribution.

At the end of June Nos 4 and 268 Squadrons left Gatwick for Odiham. Three squadrons of Spitfires (Nos 80, 229 and 274 Squadrons) arrived briefly from Merston but they had moved on again within a week. Like other airfields in the south of England, Gatwick was on the flight path of the V-1 flying bombs that were increasingly being launched against London during the summer of 1944. Balloons were erected as an attempt to disrupt the flying bombs and many of these were in the vicinity of Gatwick. This meant that flying operations were temporarily suspended until the end of August when Nos 116 and 287 Squadrons moved in. Whilst the Hurricanes of No. 116 Squadron only remained at Gatwick for little more than a week, No. 287 Squadron remained until early 1945.

Squadron	Dates at Gatwick	Aircraft Type
19 Squadron	15 – 24 Oct 43	Spitfire IX
65 Squadron	15 – 24 Oct 43	Spitfire IX
430 Squadron RCAF	15 Oct 43 – 1 Apr 44	Mustang 1
414 Squadron RCAF	3 Nov 43 – 5 Feb 44	Mustang I
168 Squadron	6 – 31 Mar 44	Mustang I
2 Squadron	4 Apr – 30 Jul 44	Mustang II
4 Squadron	4 Apr – 27 Jun 44	Spitfire XI & Mosquito XVI
268 Squadron	8 Apr – 27 Jun 44	Mustang I
80 Squadron	27 Jun – 5 Jul 44	Spitfire IX
229 Squadron	28 Jun – 1 Jul 44	Spitfire IX
274 Squadron	28 Jun – 5 Jul 44	Spitfire IX
116 Squadron	27 Aug – 5 Sep 44	Hurricane II
287 Squadron	27 Aug 44 – 20 Jan 45	Oxford, Martinet, Spitfire, Beaufighter, Tempest

With the advance into Europe going well, there was no further operational flying from Gatwick for the remainder of the war. A number of support units did, however, operate from Gatwick during late 1944 and early 1945. At the end of the war, Gatwick became a satellite airfield for Dunsfold. By then, the amount of RAF activity at the station had reduced and the station closed in 1946. The airfield was then returned to the Ministry of Civil Aviation and a number of commercial air companies operated from the site.

Gatwick was then chosen to be developed as London's second airport and all flying ceased in 1956 to start redevelopment work. The airport was re-opened by HM Queen Elizabeth II in June 1958. There were further improvements to the runway during the mid-1960s and then a major redevelopment during the late 1970s. Further expansion, including the addition of a second passenger terminal, was completed during the 1980s. The rest, as they say, is history. Gatwick is now a vast site and a major international airport. It can easily be found just to the west of Junction 9 of the M23.

Shoreham

Another Sussex airfield later to be developed as an airport is Shoreham. The airfield's origins date back to before the First World War and during the D-Day operations it was home to two Spitfire squadrons of No. 11 Group ADGB.

The airfield of Shoreham is now a municipal airport, which can be found alongside the A27 Brighton to Worthing road just one mile to the west of Shoreham-by-Sea in West Sussex. The airfield was first developed as early as 1911 and the landing ground was used by a number of early aviators for a variety of reasons. The airfield was then used by the Royal Flying Corps during the First World War but Shoreham was not retained post-war by the newly formed RAF and the land reverted to agricultural use in 1920.

As the world of aviation expanded during the inter-war years the land was eventually developed once more for private and commercial flying purposes, and eventually Shoreham became a small airport with a terminal built in 1936. With the RAF's Expansion Scheme during the mid-late 1930s as the country prepared for war, the Air Ministry became increasingly interested in the site and Shoreham was used for pilot training for the newly formed RAF Volunteer Reserve. Throughout this period Shoreham was still used for commercial aviation and indeed took on more commercial flights as the airport at Croydon became increasingly used by the RAF.

Following the outbreak of the Second World War, Shoreham's life as an airport was over; at least for the duration of the war. When the Germans advanced through France and the Low Countries in May 1940 Shoreham was taken over by the Air Ministry for Fighter Command as an advanced operating airfield for No. 11 Group. Initially Shoreham was only used by Lysanders of No. 225 Squadron for coastal patrols but then the Fighter Interception Unit moved in during August and Hurricanes of No. 422 Flight moved in during October to operate in the night-fighter role.

With the Battle of Britain over the airfield was extended to the west during 1941 and Shoreham was used by air-sea rescue and target-towing flights during 1941–2. Shoreham was used during the

The former wartime airfield of Shoreham became a municipal airport in 1971 and can be easily seen on the southern side of the A27 when heading west towards Worthing.

Dieppe Raid of 19 August 1942 when two Hurricane squadrons operated from the airfield. During 1943 Shoreham was used by units taking part in anti-aircraft practice and gunnery training, such as RAF Regiment gunners. The airfield was improved early in 1944 by a 1,200-yard runway, which was laid on what had previously been an all-grass airfield, and command and control of the airfield was passed to nearby Tangmere.

During April 1944 two Spitfire V squadrons arrived at Shoreham and for the next four months it was the busiest period of the war for the airfield. No. 277 Squadron arrived from Gravesend on 15 April and soon after No. 345 (Free French) Squadron arrived from Scotland. The Free French squadron was under the command of Commandant Bernard and had formed just two months before from French personnel transferred from North Africa. Initially the two squadrons flew defensive patrols along the coast and then started to escort light-medium bombers across to Northern France. On D-Day itself No. 345 Squadron flew sorties over the landing beaches and then later in the day escorted glider tugs across the Channel. During the next few days the squadron provided fighter cover over the beaches of Normandy, specifically over the *Utah* and *Omaha* beaches where American forces were landing.

No. 345 Squadron left Shoreham for Deanland on 16 August and was transferred to No. 141 Wing, 2nd TAF. No. 277 Squadron remained at Shoreham until it moved to Hawkinge on 5 October 1944. During the squadron's time at Shoreham it operated a number of detachments at Warmwell and Hurn as its area of operations extended westwards towards Cornwall. The airfield of Shoreham was then placed on care and maintenance, although there were brief periods of air activity until the end of the war. In 1946 Shoreham was transferred to the Ministry of Civil Aviation.

After various amounts of interest by aviation companies and businesses, Shoreham became a municipal airport in 1971. The airport is located on the western side of the River Adur and on the southern side of the A27 dual carriageway when heading west from Shoreham towards Worthing.

Squadron	Dates at Shoreham	Aircraft Type
277 Squadron	15 Apr – 5 Oct 44	Spitfire V
345 (Free French) Squadron	26 Apr – 16 Aug 44	Spitfire V

CHAPTER 7

Airfields and Advanced Landing Grounds of Surrey

Due to its geographic position and close proximity to London there have been over the years a number of sites in Surrey developed as airfields and landing grounds but only three played a part in 2nd TAF's build up to the Allied invasion of Europe and the subsequent air operations over Normandy. Two of the sites, Dunsfold and Redhill, have remained, although the site at Dunsfold is perhaps more familiar to many because of its activity with cars rather than aircraft. The third site, Horne, was only ever developed as an Advanced Landing Ground.

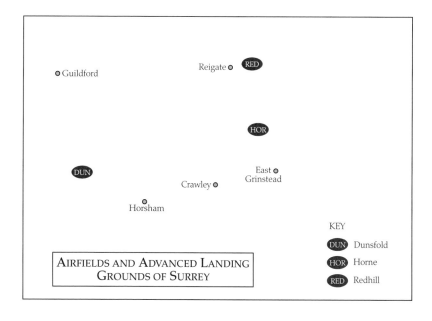

AIRFIELDS AND ADVANCED LANDING
GROUNDS OF SURREY

KEY

DUN Dunsfold
HOR Horne
RED Redhill

Dunsfold

Developed during the Second World War as an Advanced Landing Ground, Dunsfold is perhaps better know today as the home of BBC Television's Top Gear programme and the annual Wings and Wheels airshow. However, during 1943–4 Dunsfold was designated No. 139 Airfield and was home to three squadrons of Mitchell bombers of No. 2 Group, 2nd TAF.

Another of the RAF's Advanced Landing Grounds can be found at Dunsfold, 5 miles to the south-east of Godalming in Surrey. This site is also known to many for its post-war activity when it was the home of the Hawker Aircraft Company and witnessed the early development of great aircraft such as the Hunter and Harrier.

Like other ALGs in the south-east of England, the airfield was not developed until midway through the Second World War when Fighter Command was looking for additional sites that could be suitably developed for air operations. Land to the east of the village at Dunsfold was identified and work began in the spring of 1942. Construction was completed by Royal Canadian Engineers and the airfield was opened in December 1942. The layout of the airfield

Ground crew of No. 180 Squadron preparing a Mitchell for another bombing mission.

included three standard runways, laid out in a triangular pattern, with aircraft dispersals on the southern and eastern sides of the airfield.

Having been built by Canadian Engineers, it was appropriate that the first units to move into Dunsfold were all Canadian. No. 39 Wing RCAF was an army cooperation wing and its three squadrons were to be the first resident units at the new airfield. The first to arrive was No. 400 Squadron RCAF, which arrived on 4 December 1942, followed the next day by No. 414 Squadron RCAF. Equipped essentially with Mustang 1 aircraft, although No. 400 Squadron still operated some Tomahawks, the role of the squadrons was to carry out army cooperation duties and both squadrons commenced reconnaissance and ground-attack missions across the Channel in France. The Wing's third squadron, No. 430 Squadron RCAF, moved into Dunsfold on 11 January 1943. Unlike its fellow squadrons, which had both been in existence since 1941, No. 430 Squadron had only just formed at Hartfordbridge the week before and Dunsfold was its first home. The squadron initially received some Tomahawks to start its work-up training but soon started to take delivery of Mustangs for operations and the squadron flew its first operational sorties from Dunsfold on 26 May.

Army Cooperation Command ceased to exist on 1 June 1943 and Dunsfold then became a fighter station and began preparations for the formation of 2nd TAF. The three Canadian squadrons all moved out in July. Nos 414 and 430 Squadrons moved to Gatwick and the last to leave was No. 400 Squadron, which moved to Woodchurch on 28 July. As part of the scheme of numbering airfields, Dunsfold initially became No. 128 Airfield, although this number was soon passed to Woodchurch. With no resident squadrons, there then followed a period of relative quiet at Dunsfold before Mitchell bombers of Nos 98 and 180 Squadrons moved in from Foulsham on 18 August. Unlike many fighter squadrons, which were frequently moved in and out of airfields and often had several homes in any given period, these two medium bomber squadrons were able to enjoy the stability of making Dunsfold their home; indeed, apart from an occasional short detachment during early 1944, the two squadrons would remain at Dunsfold until the Allied advance into Europe was fully underway more than a year later.

On 26 November the two Dunsfold squadrons took part in an attack against a V-weapon site at Martinvast. The attack took place during the afternoon and the target was strongly defended. Three

Mitchells from No. 180 Squadron were shot down with the loss of all the crews; it was a devastating blow to those at Dunsfold at the time. On 22 December Nos 98 and 180 Squadrons took part in the largest operation by No. 2 Group against 'Noball' sites. Each squadron provided twelve Mitchells and the task of the Dunsfold squadrons was to attack the site at St Pierre des Jonquières; elsewhere, thirty-six Bostons from Hartfordbridge attacked the site at Mesnil Allard. The following day No. 320 Squadron joined forces with No. 226 Squadron from Swanton Morley to attack Puchervin, whilst Nos 98 and 180 Squadrons again returned to St Pierre des Jonquières. All the Mitchells returned safely to Dunsfold.

Dunsfold was renumbered as No. 139 Airfield and during the winter the two squadrons continued to carry out various sorties, including attacks against V-1 sites across the Channel. No. 98 Squadron became the first unit within No. 2 Group to use the new navigation equipment *Gee*, which was fitted to its Mitchells during February 1944. On 18 February the two squadrons were joined by No. 320 (Dutch) Squadron, also equipped with Mitchell II bombers, which completed the wing under the command of No. 2 Group. On

A Mitchell of No. 180 Squadron, which was one of three Mitchell squadrons to operate from Dunsfold during the D-Day operations.

25 February the Mitchells of No. 320 Squadron joined forces with Mitchells from No. 226 Squadron at Hartfordbridge to attack a 'Noball' site near Abbeville. Despite the target being heavily defended, all No. 320 Squadron's Mitchells returned safely to Dunsfold, although No. 226 Squadron suffered badly; two Mitchells were shot down and another force-landed back in England.

The Mitchells of Dunsfold continued their attacks against 'Noball' sites. On 18 March both Nos 98 and 320 Squadrons provided aircraft for an attack against a site at Gorenflos. Although two aircraft from No. 320 Squadron were badly hit, both aircraft managed to make it away from the target where they soon reached the relatively less-hostile English Channel; both aircraft ditched safely and all eight crew members were safely picked up. The squadron was not so lucky just two days later when one of its aircraft was shot down near Flixecourt; the crew on this occasion were all killed. No. 98 Squadron also suffered a loss on the same raid when one of its aircraft was hit by ground defences. Although this aircraft managed to make it away from the target and out to sea where it ditched to the west of Boulougne, the crew were all killed. It was another bad day for Dunsfold.

Throughout April the Mitchell crews of the Dunsfold squadrons continued their attacks, almost daily. There had been an enormous effort against the 'Noball' sites and the Dunsfold crews had undoubtedly played their part, often at considerable cost. As the Allied invasion plans were starting to take more shape, the number of attacks against these sites decreased as other targets became a higher priority. There was now also increasing support from the medium bombers of the American Ninth Air Force. However, there were still further attacks against 'Noball' sites. During one such attack at Bois Coquerel during the late afternoon of 8 May, No. 98 Squadron suffered a significant loss when the Mitchell captained by the squadron commander, Wing Commander R.K.F. Bell-Irving, was hit by flak and crashed to the south of Abbeville; the crew of four were all killed. Command of the squadron was then passed to Wing Commander J.G.C. Paul the following week.

Dunsfold then became No. 139 Wing. For the Mitchell crews, their targets now included railways, in particular the stations, junctions and marshalling yards. The bombing effort was quite deliberately spread over a wide area in northern France so that there were no clues whatsoever as to where the final invasion area would be. As D-Day got closer, the attacks became more focussed but, again, without giving Normandy away as the designated area for the Allied landings. By attacking the railway junctions and marshalling yards, the plan was to deny the Germans the chance of rapidly reinforcing positions once the invasion had taken place. On the eve of D-Day, Dunsfold's Mitchells were involved in the bombing of targets in the area of Caen. Following the D-Day landings of 6 June, the Mitchells took part in nightly attacks against enemy communications networks. As the Allies started to breakout of Normandy the Mitchells began to attack other targets, such as ammunition dumps and fuel installations. The squadrons were also involved in support of Operation *Market*, the aerial assault on Arnhem, in September. During these air operations, No. 98 Squadron lost two Mitchells; the first medium bomber losses since the formation of 2nd TAF nearly a year earlier.

In October it was decided to move a number of Mitchell squadrons across the Channel and No. 139 Wing was the first to go, leaving Dunsfold for B.58 Melsbroek on 18 October. Dunsfold was then placed on care and maintenance until January 1945 when the airfield became a satellite airfield for Odiham. No. 83 Group

A memorial to those who served at Dunsfold was funded by the public and unveiled in 1992. It can be found outside the Alfold Barn pub at Alfold Crossways on the A281.

Support Unit operated from Dunsfold with aircraft such as Spitfires, Typhoons and Tempests. Otherwise, there was little or no air activity until the end of the war when Dunsfold was used as a landing ground for DC3 Dakotas bringing back prisoners of war from the continent. This was a huge task and Dunsfold often received well over 100 aircraft a day during May. This continued well into June by which time well over 50,000 former prisoners of war had passed through Dunsfold. The airfield was also used as No. 83 Group's Disbandment Centre with the task of receiving overseas units that had disbanded at the end of the war. In September 1945 Dunsfold was briefly home to the Spitfires of No. 16 Squadron, which had just returned from their previous base at Eindhoven in Holland. By the end of October the squadron had gone and the airfield was placed on care and maintenance once more.

Dunsfold was then leased by Skyway Ltd, which operated a fleet of transport aircraft including Yorks, Lancastrians and Dakotas. Dunsfold became the company's main operating base and it played a major part in air operations during the Berlin Airlift of 1948–9. With the Berlin Airlift over, the airfield was acquired by the Hawker Aircraft Company in 1950. For the next forty years Dunsfold was a busy place with the development of new aircraft such as the

The former wartime airfield is now Dunsfold Park and is familiar to many TV viewers as the location for the BBC's Top Gear programme.

Hawker Hunter, which first flew from Dunsfold in May 1953. In October 1960 the company, which was then Hawker Siddeley, had the first test flight of its Hawker P1127 prototype; this was the development aircraft that led to the Harrier, the first vertical take-off and landing (VTOL) jet fighter. In 1977 Hawker Siddeley became part of British Aerospace and the airfield was eventually closed in 2000, with the company's development and manufacturing moving to other sites. British Aerospace itself was renamed BAE Systems and in 2002 the airfield was bought by the Rutland Group and the Royal Bank of Scotland to become known as Dunsfold Park.

The airfield is now familiar to millions of TV viewers, as Dunsfold Park is where the BBC records its television programme Top Gear, using a former hangar as a studio and the runway and taxiways as a test track. The site was also used to film scenes for the James Bond film Casino Royale. Dunsfold Park is currently home to more than 100 businesses, home to the Surrey Air Ambulance Service and also to Wings and Wheels, a combined air and motor show held annually in August; the first Wings and Wheels was held in 2005 and in 2008 the event was attended by an estimated 20,000 people. In recent years a proposal has been put forward to use the land for the development of a new eco-village with more than 2,000 homes and other facilities to be built on the site but, as yet, the proposal has not gained approval.

The airfield can be found by taking the A281 westwards from Horsham or southwards from Guildford. When travelling from the direction of Guildford take the B2130 south-westwards from the A281 towards the villages of Loxhill and Dunsfold. After just over a mile there is a sharp right-hand bend; the B2130 continues to Loxhill but the minor road to the left, called Stovolds Hill, leads to the airfield at Dunsfold Park. There is a local museum on the site, which is run by Reg Day, a former wartime member of Dunsfold. The museum is open on Wednesdays only. There is also a memorial outside the Alfold Barn pub on the A281 at Alfold Crossways. The memorial was funded by public money and was unveiled on 20 July 1992, fifty years to the day after the first aircraft, a Tiger Moth of the RCAF, landed at Dunsfold.

Squadron	Dates at Dunsfold	Aircraft Type
98 Squadron	18 Aug 1943 – 18 Oct 1944	Mitchell II
180 Squadron	18 Aug 1943 – 16 Oct 1944	Mitchell II
320 Squadron	18 Feb – 18 Oct 1944	Mitchell II

Horne

Another relatively unknown Advanced Landing Ground in Surrey is Horne. It was only used for a very short period of the Second World War and on D-Day was home to Spitfires of No. 142 Wing of No. 85 Group, 2nd TAF. After the war the land reverted to agriculture.

Another airfield to have only existed for a short period was the airfield of Horne, which was developed as an Advanced Landing Ground. The airfield was only ever grass and had two runways of 1,400 yards in length, one ran from the south-west to the north-east and the other ran from the south-east to the north-west. Horne was only used operationally for a very short period of the war when it was used during the build-up to D-Day and the subsequent breakout of Normandy; three Spitfire squadrons of No. 142 Wing operated from the airfield during May and June 1944.

The facilities at the Advanced Landing Grounds were very basic and the ground crew often worked out of tents next to the aircraft parked on the metal tracking.

The three Spitfire squadrons all arrived on 30 April 1944. No. 130 Squadron, under the command of Squadron Leader Bill Ireson, arrived from Lympne. They were joined by the Polish unit, No. 303 Squadron under the command of Squadron Leader Tadeusz Koc, which arrived from Ballyhalbert. Like many other Polish airmen, Tadeusz Koc had fought against the *Luftwaffe* during the German invasion of Poland in September 1939; indeed, he was credited with his country's last kill before Poland fell. He eventually found his way to England and flew with Nos 317 and 308 Squadrons, during which time he was awarded the DFC, before he was given command of No. 303 Squadron in November 1943.

The third squadron to arrive at Horne, and complete the international flavour there, was the Canadian unit No. 402 Squadron RCAF under the command of the Canadian ace Squadron Leader Geoff Northcott. Born in Manitoba, Northcott joined the RCAF in 1940. He initially served as a sergeant pilot and was commissioned at the end of 1941. Northcott was then posted to No. 603 Squadron where he flew Spitfires from Ta Kali during the defence of Malta. He later returned to the UK and was given

A plaque is situated in a clump of trees in Bones Lane and marks the site of the former airfield of Horne.

The plaque was unveiled in 1994 to commemorate the squadrons and personnel that served at Horne during the Second World War.

command of No. 402 Squadron RCAF in June 1943. During his time in command of the squadron, Northcott enjoyed considerable successes in the air. By the time he arrived at Horne he had been credited with seven kills and many more were shared, probably destroyed or damaged. He had been awarded the DFC and bar, and he would later add a DSO to his achievements on leaving Horne.

During the final build-up to D-Day the Horne squadrons were mainly involved in *Ramrod* missions but on D-Day itself the squadrons mainly provided low-level fighter cover over the Normandy beaches and some shipping patrols as well; these missions were continued during the immediate days after D-Day, although the occasional bomber escort mission was flown as well. By 19 June all three squadrons had left Horne for Westhampnett.

The site has reverted to agriculture and there is also a golf course. In 1994 a plaque was unveiled by Horne Parish Council in its centenary year to commemorate the three squadrons and personnel that served at Horne as part of No. 142 Wing during the Second World War and, in particular, the part played by the wing during the D-Day operations.

The village of Horne and site of the former airfield is in Surrey between Redhill and East Grinstead, to the west of the A22. When heading south along the A22 from Junction 6 of the M25, after 4

Looking in a southerly direction across the site of the former airfield at Horne. The area is now overflown by aircraft making their final approach into Gatwick Airport.

miles take a right turn straight to Horne. When heading north from the A22 junction with the A264 just after East Grinstead, after 2 miles turn left at Newchapel on the B2028 and then after a mile turn right for the village of Horne. The site of the former airfield is just to the south of the golf course. The best way to find it from the village of Horne is to leave the village southwards along Church Road. At the T-junction turn left into Croydonbarn Lane. After about 400 yards, and immediately before the golf club, turn right into Bones Lane. After just over half a mile you will notice open fields to the left and right of Bones Lane. Stop at the next clump of trees on your left where you will see the plaque. This is a good place to view the site of the former airfield. Without knowing the precise location of the plaque, it is not easy to find but hopefully these directions will help you.

Squadron	Dates at Horne	Aircraft Type
130 Squadron	30 Apr – 19 Jun 44	Spitfire V
303 'Warsaw-Kosciusco' Squadron	30 Apr – 18 Jun 44	Spitfire V
402 Squadron RCAF	30 Apr – 19 Jun 44	Spitfire V

Redhill

Now the site of Redhill Aerodrome, the origins of this airfield date back to the 1930s. Following the formation of 2nd TAF in November 1943 Redhill was designated No. 128 Airfield and was home to two squadrons of Mustangs of No. 83 Group.

The airfield at Redhill still remains in use today and is now called the Redhill Aerodrome. It lies 3 miles to the east of Reigate in Surrey. The airfield was first developed in 1934 to accommodate the Redhill Flying Club and was first used by the RAF in 1937 as a flying training school. Just after the outbreak of the Second World War Redhill became a satellite for Kenley. For the early weeks of the Battle of Britain there were no resident squadrons at Redhill, and the airfield was only used for emergencies, but during the latter period of the battle Redhill was home to two squadrons.

The first squadron to arrive at Redhill was No. 600 Squadron, which was equipped with Blenheims and arrived from Hornchurch

Redhill was home to a Support Unit of No. 83 Group during the spring of 1944 and many aircraft passed through the airfield on their way to the frontline units of 2nd TAF.

on 12 September 1940. During its brief stay of just a month the squadron was mainly employed in the night-fighter role, although its period of operations proved frustrating as there were no successes; it was early days for the Blenheim's radar. The squadron was replaced by No. 219 Squadron, also equipped with Blenheims, but this squadron soon started to take delivery of Beaufighters. The story for No. 219 Squadron was much the same as with No. 600 Squadron, frustrating with no successes in terms of enemy aircraft destroyed.

After the Battle of Britain Redhill was further developed and was used by many fighter squadrons, most of which operated the Spitfire V. There were too many movements to mention and the squadrons' period of operation from Redhill ranged from a matter of days to a few months. Although the two runways remained grass there was a perimeter track, aircraft dispersal pens and blister hangars constructed. Redhill was used during the famous Dieppe Raid on 19 August 1942. On this occasion the airfield was briefly home to five multi-national Spitfires squadrons: No. 303 Squadron (Polish), Nos 310 and 312 Squadrons (Czech), No. 350 Squadron (Belgian) and No. 611 Squadron (British). The squadrons had a most successful day, claiming at least sixteen enemy aircraft destroyed between them, with several more damaged, for the loss of just two pilots.

Many squadrons came and went during 1943 but the only long-term residents during the winter of 1943–4 were the Canadians of No. 400 RCAF Squadron. When the squadron arrived at Redhill from Woodchurch on 15 October 1943 it was equipped with Mustang Is. No. 400 Squadron RCAF flew its last operational sorties with its Mustang Is on 3 January 1944 when it took part in photo-reconnaissance duties over the Cabourg area; sadly, one of it pilots was killed. The next day the squadron started to take delivery of Spitfire XIs and Mosquito XVIs. On 18 February the squadron moved to Odiham.

This left Redhill with no resident squadrons during the build up to D-Day but the airfield did become home to a support unit of No. 83 Group, 2nd TAF, and various other second-line units. As D-Day approached No. 83 Group Support Unit became increasingly busy preparing Spitfires for issue to the front-line squadrons. The workload for the unit's personnel was particularly busy during May when literally dozens and dozens of Spitfires passed through

Looking across Redhill airfield, which in areas has remained generally unchanged.

Redhill for either repairs or routine maintenance before being returned to their former unit or moved on to another.

On 5 September 1944 No. 116 Squadron moved into Redhill. This squadron was equipped with various aircraft types, including Tiger Moths and Oxfords, and its main role was to calibrate the radars used by anti-aircraft defences. In January 1945 No. 287 Squadron arrived from Gatwick; this unit also flew a variety of types, including Spitfires and Tempests, again in the anti-aircraft cooperation role. Both squadrons moved out of Redhill at the end of the war.

After the Second World War, Redhill was used as a reserve flying school and for civil aviation until 1954. Flying then ceased for economical reasons for a few years but resumed again in 1959. The following year Bristow Helicopters moved in and remained until 1998, using the airfield for the training of its pilots and engineers; after the helicopters left the head office of Bristow remained at Redhill until 2004. Proposals to further develop the site for larger commercial purposes, which included building a new terminal to

Redhill Aerodrome today.

handle 15 million passengers a year, seem to have come to nothing. The airfield is now operated by Redhill Aerodrome Limited and is used by helicopters and civilian aircraft.

The airfield can be found to the south-east of the town of Redhill, to the south of the A25 Redhill to Oxted road and to the east of the A23 Redhill to Horley road; the M23 runs north-south to the western side of the airfield. Redhill is not a particularly easy airfield to find if you are unfamiliar with the area but is to the south of the village of South Nutfield, which is not far from Bletchingley on the A25.

From Redhill take the A25 eastwards towards Bletchingley. After about 2 miles turn right into Fullers Wood Lane, which then becomes Clay Lane, towards the village of South Nutfield. Just before the village of South Nutfield turn right into Kings Mill Lane and this leads to the aerodrome. The address is: Redhill Aerodrome Limited, Terminal Building, Redhill Aerodrome, Surrey, RH1 5YP.

Squadron	Dates at Redhill	Aircraft Type
400 Squadron RCAF	15 Oct 43 – 18 Feb 44	Mustang I, Spitfire XI & Mosquito XVI

2nd TAF Orbat – 30 November 1943

2nd TAF Headquarters
34 Wing – Hartford Bridge

No. 16 Squadron   Spitfire XI
No. 140 Squadron   Spitfire XI

No. 2 Group
Headquarters – Bylaugh Hall, East Dereham

No. 137 Airfield	Hartford Bridge	No. 88 Squadron	Boston III
		No. 107 Squadron	Boston III
		No. 342 Squadron	Boston III
No. 138 Airfield	Lasham	No. 320 Squadron	Mitchell II
		No. 613 Squadron	Mosquito VI
No. 139 Airfield	Dunsfold	No. 98 Squadron	Mitchell II
		No. 180 Squadron	Mitchell II
No. 140 Airfield	Sculthorpe	No. 21 Squadron	Mosquito VI
		No. 464 Squadron RAAF	Mosquito VI
		No. 487 Squadron RNZAF	Mosquito VI
No designated number	Swanton Morley	No. 226 Squadron	Mitchell II

No. 83 Group
Headquarters – Gatton Park, Reigate

No. 15 Wing	No. 122 Airfield	Gravesend	No. 19 Squadron	Spitfire IX
			No. 65 Squadron	Spitfire IX
			No. 122 Squadron	Spitfire IX
	No. 125 Airfield	Detling	No. 132 Squadron	Spitfire IX
			No. 184 Squadron	Hurricane IV
			No. 602 Squadron	Spitfire IX
No. 16 Wing	No. 121 Airfield	Westhampnett	No. 174 Squadron	Typhoon I
			No. 175 Squadron	Typhoon I
			No. 245 Squadron	Typhoon I
	No. 124 Airfield	Merston	No. 181 Squadron	Typhoon I
			No. 182 Squadron	Typhoon I
			No. 247 Squadron	Typhoon I
No. 17 Wing	No. 126 Airfield	Biggin Hill	No. 401 Squadron RCAF	Spitfire IX
			No. 411 Squadron RCAF	Spitfire V
			No. 412 Squadron RCAF	Spitfire IX
	No. 127 Airfield	Kenley	No. 403 Squadron RCAF	Spitfire IX
			No. 421 Squadron RCAF	Spitfire IX
	No. 128 Airfield	Redhill	No. 231 Squadron	Mustang I
			No. 400 Squadron RCAF	Mustang I
	No. 129 Airfield	Gatwick	No. 414 Squadron RCAF	Mustang I
			No. 430 Squadron RCAF	Mustang I

In addition, there were four Army Observation Post squadrons allocated to No. 83 Group. These squadrons were equipped with Auster IIIs and were: No. 653 Squadron (Penshurst), No. 658 Squadron (Clifton), No. 659 Squadron (Clifton) and No. 662 Squadron (Old Sarum).

No. 84 Group
Headquarters – Cowley Barracks, Oxford

No. 18 Wing	No. 131 Airfield	Northolt	No. 302 Squadron	Spitfire IX
			No. 308 Squadron	Spitfire IX
			No. 317 Squadron	Spitfire IX
	No. 133 Airfield	Heston	No. 306 Squadron	Spitfire V
			No. 315 Squadron	Spitfire V
No. 19 Wing	No. 132 Airfield	North Weald	No. 331 Squadron	Spitfire IX
			No. 332 Squadron	Spitfire IX
	No. 134 Airfield	Ibsley	No. 310 Squadron	Spitfire V
			No. 312 Squadron	Spitfire V
			No. 313 Squadron	Spitfire V
No. 20 Wing	No. 135 Airfield	Hornchurch	No. 66 Squadron	Spitfire IX
			No. 129 Squadron	Spitfire IX
			No. 350 Squadron	Spitfire IX
	No. 136 Airfield	Fairlop	No. 164 Squadron	Hurricane IV
			No. 195 Squadron	Typhoon I
	No. 123 Airfield	Thruxton	No. 63 Squadron	Mustang I
			No. 168 Squadron	Mustang I
			No. 170 Squadron	Mustang I
	No. 130 Airfield	Odiham	No. 2 Squadron	Mustang I
			No. 4 Squadron	Mustang I

In addition, there were three Army Observation Post squadrons allocated to No. 84 Group. These squadrons were equipped with Auster IIIs and were: No. 652 Squadron (Ipswich), No. 660 Squadron (Hammerwood House) and No. 661 Squadron (Andover).

2nd TAF Orbat – 6 June 1944

2nd TAF Headquarters
34 (PR) Wing Northolt

No. 16 Squadron	Spitfire XI
No. 69 Squadron	Wellington XIII
No. 140 Squadron	Mosquito XVI

In addition, No. 1401 (Met) Flight based at Manston

No. 2 Group

No. 137 Wing	Hartford Bridge	No. 88 Squadron	Boston III
		No. 226 Squadron	Mitchell II
		No. 342 Squadron	Boston III
No. 138 Wing	Lasham	No. 107 Squadron	Mosquito VI
		No. 305 Squadron	Mosquito VI
		No. 613 Squadron	Mosquito VI
No. 139 Wing	Dunsfold	No. 98 Squadron	Mitchell II
		No. 180 Squadron	Mitchell II
		No. 320 Squadron	Mitchell II
No. 140 Wing	Hunsdon	No. 21 Squadron	Mosquito VI
		No. 464 Squadron RAAF	Mosquito VI
		No. 487 Squadron RNZAF	Mosquito VI

No. 83 Group

No. 121 Wing	Holmsley South	No. 174 Squadron	Typhoon I
		No. 175 Squadron	
		No. 245 Squadron	
No. 122 Wing	Funtington	No. 19 Squadron	Mustang III
		No. 65 Squadron	
		No. 122 Squadron	
No. 124 Wing	Hurn	No. 181 Squadron	
		No. 182 Squadron	
		No. 247 Squadron	Typhoon I
No. 143 Wing	Hurn	No. 438 Squadron	
		No. 439 Squadron	
		No. 440 Squadron	
No. 125 Wing	Ford	No. 132 Squadron	
		No. 453 Squadron RAAF	
		No. 602 Squadron	Spitfire IX
No. 144 Wing	Ford	No. 441 Squadron	
		No. 442 Squadron	
		No. 443 Squadron	
No. 126 Wing	Tangmere	No. 401 Squadron	
		No. 411 Squadron	
		No. 412 Squadron	Spitfire IX
No. 127 Wing	Tangmere	No. 403 Squadron	
		No. 416 Squadron	
		No. 421 Squadron	
No. 129 Wing	Westhampnett	No. 184 Squadron	Typhoon I
No. 39 (PR) Wing	Odiham	No. 168 Squadron	
		No. 414 Squadron	Mustang I
		No. 430 Squadron	
		No. 400 Squadron	Spitfire XI

In addition, there were four Army Observation Post squadrons allocated to No. 83 Group. These squadrons were equipped with Auster IVs and were: No. 653 Squadron (Penshurst), No. 658 Squadron (Old Sarum), No. 659 Squadron (East Grinstead) and No. 662 Squadron (Old Sarum).

No. 84 Group

Wing	Airfield	Squadron	Aircraft
No. 123 Wing	Thorney Island	No. 198 Squadron	Typhoon I
		No. 609 Squadron	
No. 136 Wing		No. 164 Squadron	
		No. 184 Squadron	
No. 131 Wing	Chailey	No. 302 Squadron	Spitfire IX
		No. 308 Squadron	
		No. 317 Squadron	
No. 132 Wing	Bognor Regis	No. 66 Squadron	Spitfire IX
		No. 331 Squadron	
		No. 332 Squadron	
No. 133 Wing	Coolham	No. 129 Squadron	Mustang III
		No. 306 Squadron RAAF	
		No. 315 Squadron	
No. 134 Wing	Appledram	No. 310 Squadron	Spitfire IX
		No. 312 Squadron	
		No. 313 Squadron	
No. 135 Wing	Selsey	No. 222 Squadron	Spitfire IX
		No. 349 Squadron	
		No. 485 Squadron	
No. 145 Wing	Merston	No. 329 Squadron	Spitfire IX
		No. 340 Squadron	
		No. 341 Squadron	
No. 146 Wing	Needs Oar Point	No. 193 Squadron	Typhoon I
		No. 197 Squadron	
		No. 257 Squadron	
		No. 266 Squadron	
No. 35 (Recce) Wing	Gatwick	No. 2 Squadron	Mustang I
		No. 268 Squadron	
		No. 4 Squadron	Spitfire XI

In addition, there were three Army Observation Post squadrons allocated to No. 84 Group. These squadrons were equipped with Auster IVs and were: No. 652 Squadron (Cobham), No. 660 Squadron (Westenhanger) and No. 661 Squadron (Biggin Hill & Fairchildes).

No. 85 Group

No. 141 Wing	Hartford Bridge	No. 264 Squadron	Mosquito XIII
		No. 410 Squadron	
		No. 322 Squadron	Spitfire XIV
No. 142 Wing	Horne	No. 130 Squadron	Spitfire V
		No. 303 Squadron	
		No. 402 Squadron RCAF	
No. 147 Wing	Zeals	No. 488 Squadron	Mosquito XIII
		No. 604 Squadron	
No. 148 Wing	West Malling	No. 29 Squadron	Mosquito XIII
		No. 409 Squadron	
		No. 91 Squadron	Spitfire XIV
No. 150 Wing	Newchurch	No. 3 Squadron	Tempest V
		No. 486 Squadron	
		No. 56 Squadron	Spitfire IX

There were also two RAF Air Spotting Pool squadrons allocated to No. 85 Group. The two RAF squadrons were No. 26 Squadron and No. 63 Squadron, equipped with Spitfire Vs and based at Lee-on-Solent. Also based at Lee-on-Solent for this task were various Fleet Air Arm squadrons.

In addition to the air assets of 2nd TAF there were units and airfields of the RAF's Air Defence of Great Britain and the US Ninth Air Force supporting the D-Day air operations and the subsequent Allied breakout of Normandy. The RAF's ADGB airfields and units in East Anglia and the South-East were:

11 Group ADGB

Bradwell Bay	219 Squadron	Mosquito XVII
	278 Squadron	Warwick & Anson
Deanland	64 Squadron	Spitfire V & Spitfire IX
	234 Squadron	611 Squadron
Detling	80 Squadron	Spitfire IX
	229 Squadron	
	274 Squadron	
Friston	350 (Belgian) Squadron	Spitfire V
	501 Squadron	
	303 'Warsaw-Kosciusco' Squadron	
	402 Squadron RCAF	
Lympne	33 Squadron	Spitfire IX
	74 Squadron	
	127 Squadron	
Manston	137 Squadron	Typhoon I
	143 Squadron	Beaufighter X
	605 Squadron	Mosquito VI
Shoreham	277 Squadron	Spitfire V
	345 (Free French) Squadron	Spitfire V
West Malling	29 Squadron	Mosquito XII & XIII
	91 Squadron	Spitfire XIV
	96 Squadron	Mosquito XIII
	409 Squadron RCAF	Mosquito XIII